UNITED NATIONS CONFERENCE ON TRADE AND DEVELOPMENT

empretec

Women in Business

Building purpose-driven enterprises amid crises

United Nations

United Nations Publications
405 East 42nd Street
New York, New York 10017
United States of America

Email: publications@un.org

Website: https://shop.un.org/

This publication has been edited externally.

United Nations publication issued by the United Nations Conference on Trade and Development

UNCTAD/DIAE/ED/2022/1

ISBN: 978-92-1-113077-5
eISBN: 978-92-1-002202-6
Sales No. 22.II.D.46

Acknowledgements

This publication was prepared under the overall guidance of James Zhan, Director, Division on Investment and Enterprise, UNCTAD. The team was led by UNCTAD's entrepreneurship chief, Arlette Verploegh and included Lorenzo Tosini, Maha Alanazi, Zarja Vojta, Peter Navarrette and Dorothy Dillard. Contributions and comments were provided by Irais Martinez.

The content of this publication is based on interviews carried out by Dr. Chandra Vadhana Radhakrishnan, an Empreteca, and her team at Prayaana Labs. She worked in conjunction with a group of women entrepreneurs selected for Empretec Women in Business Awards throughout the years, since its inception in 2008.

The stories and publication were written and edited by Amy Shelver.

The design, layout and formatting were provided by Nicholas Symes.

This publication was prepared with a financial contribution from the UNDA project, "The Global Initiative towards post-Covid-19 resurgence of the MSME sector".

Contents

Preface

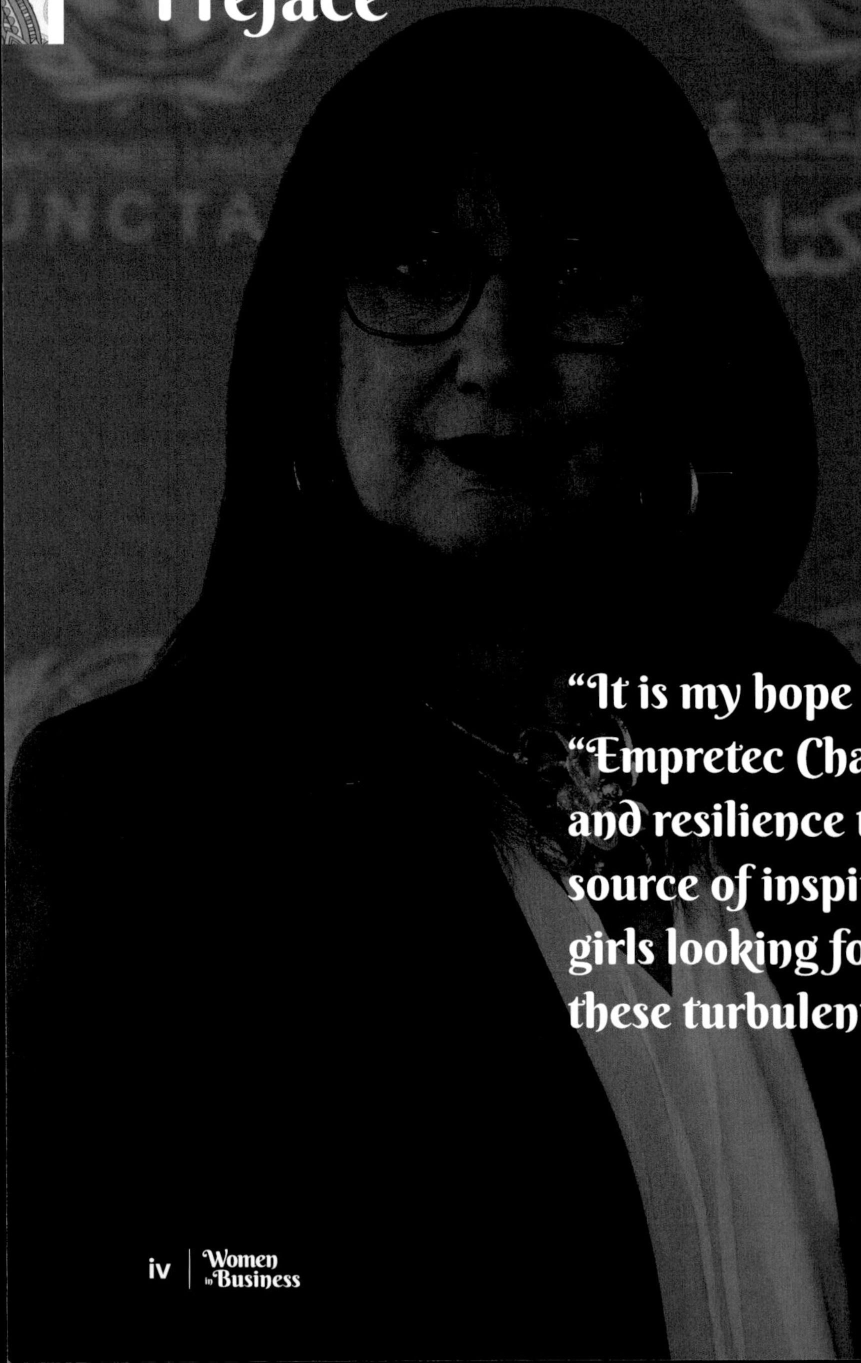

"It is my hope that the stories of these 21 "Empretec Champions" and the ingenuity and resilience they display amid crises, is a source of inspiration for other women and girls looking for role models and hope in these turbulent times."

REBECA GRYNSPAN
Secretary-General
UNCTAD

A third of all entrepreneurs in the world are women. Their contribution to development is clear: as their business grow, they inspire, create jobs, and offer themselves, their families, and their communities a chance for a better, more inclusive future.

There are, however, two problems. First, a third is still too low – there are two men entrepreneurs for every woman entrepreneur. And second, women businesses are relatively smaller, more fragile, and slower to grow. This is due to the multiple and intersectional challenges that limit women's potential, and that require bold and collective action to be overcome.

That is the main goal of UNCTAD´s Empretec Programme: to support women entrepreneurs, especially in developing countries, reach their full potential. We do this by offering them a wealth of more than 34 years of experience in capacity building, skill development, and business transformation.

The Women in Business award is part of our Empretec Programme. Through it, we seek to recognize women who have gone through our programme and have shown outstanding performance and success. This year, Women in Business celebrates 21 women who have exhibited incredible resilience in what have been extremely challenging years. With this award, we want to highlight their creativity, their commitment and their strength to challenge gender stereotypes and become forces of change and development within their communities.

The success stories included in this edition showcase women breaking into what had been considered men dominated industries, like mechanics, agriculture, security, and construction.

Through them, we learn how women entrepreneurs can face and defeat prejudice with professionalism, technical skill training and advisory. And how women-led businesses can be scaled-up to large-sized companies, and what it takes to succeed in doing that.

These 21 inspirational stories are part of a network of over 72 Empretec women champions, from 31 countries over seven editions of our awards. For many, the Women in Business recognition has been life-changing and game-changing. It is my hope that the stories included in this book and the ingenuity and resilience they display amid crises, is a source of inspiration for other women and girls looking for role models and hope in these turbulent times.

Our Empretec Champions are living proof that with the right support system and perseverance, we – women – can be agents of change, realize our dreams and the dreams of the 2030 Agenda.

The need for ideas, inspiration and role models has never been more urgent as we seek hope and meaning amid waves of crises. During COVID-19, and generally in crises, women have stood out as caregivers, innovators, community leaders and providers.

Women tend to be more resilient in times of trial and often pick up more responsibility.

This is not a novel phenomenon. Women who break glass ceilings and create new pathways for themselves face daily challenges.

The stories presented here are emblematic of the power and creativity of women entrepreneurs. It demonstrates their strength. It charts their experiences. It underscores their commitment to making a difference. And it shows how the landscape of entrepreneurship is changing.

It showcases how entrepreneurship is becoming more inclusive, equal, representative, and sustainable because of women in business.

But it also underscores the importance of supporting women entrepreneurs and business owners as key to delivering on several of the global goals.

Amid crises it is still crucial that we focus on scoring the sustainable development goals through purpose-driven businesses, human-centered outcomes which deliver real social impact, good jobs, solid opportunities, sustainable business models, and concern and care for the people and the planet.

WHAT IS EMPRETEC?

Empretec is the UN Conference on Trade and Development's (UNCTAD) flagship capacity-building programme for entrepreneurs and small business owners. It is a global initiative coordinated from Geneva, Switzerland.

The programme primarily aims to promote entrepreneurship. But it is also focused on ensuring that developing countries' productive capacities – the resources, entrepreneurial capabilities and production linkages that together determine a country's ability to produce goods and services that will help it grow and develop – are enhanced. The Empretec programme also works to boost the international competitiveness of micro, small and medium-sized enterprises (MSMEs) and start-ups in both developing countries and economies in transition.

The Empretec programme is delivered through a unique and strong global network of national business development centres in 41 countries. This powerful network is the foundation of Empretec. It acts as a platform for information, knowledge sharing, mentorship and support, while promoting entrepreneurship at all levels.

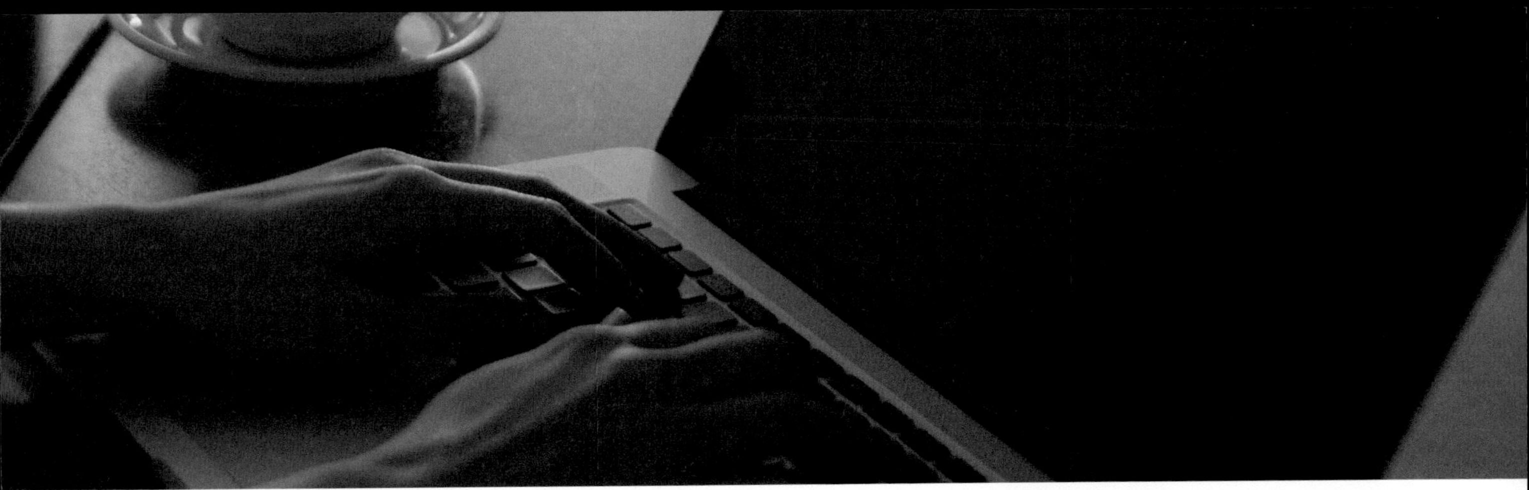

The Empretec programme is part of UNCTAD's 360 degree approach to entrepreneurship development. Since its inception in Argentina in 1988, it recently moved to Empretec 2.0 so as to be better equipped to meet the challenges of a changing landscape in the world of entrepreneurship.

The new version emphasises on the transformative power of entrepreneurs, introduces innovative features and the use of modern technologies in daily operations, elevates and expands the global aspect of the programme and strengthens its activities towards different types of entrepreneurs.

One of Empretec's core products, the Entrepreneurship Training Workshop (ETW), promotes a methodology of behavioural change that helps entrepreneurs put their ideas into action and aids fledgling businesses to grow.

It is a unique, competencies and behavioural based approach to developing successful entrepreneurs, changing their mindset, and enhancing the productive capacity and international competitiveness of MSMEs.

The UN formally recognized entrepreneurship as a key ingredient in development through a series of General Assembly resolutions on entrepreneurship for sustainable development since 2012. It helps them establish and expand businesses, creating thousands of jobs in the process.

Specifically, the recent United Nations General Assembly Resolution A/RES/73/225 acknowledges the value of UNCTAD's Empretec programme and encourages member States to invest in entrepreneurship and skills development. Its mandate is to facilitate sustainable development and inclusive growth.

The main beneficiaries are entrepreneurs, aspiring entrepreneurs, small and microbusinesses (including local small suppliers), start-ups, low literate groups, young people and intrapreneurs at managerial level in decision-making positions.

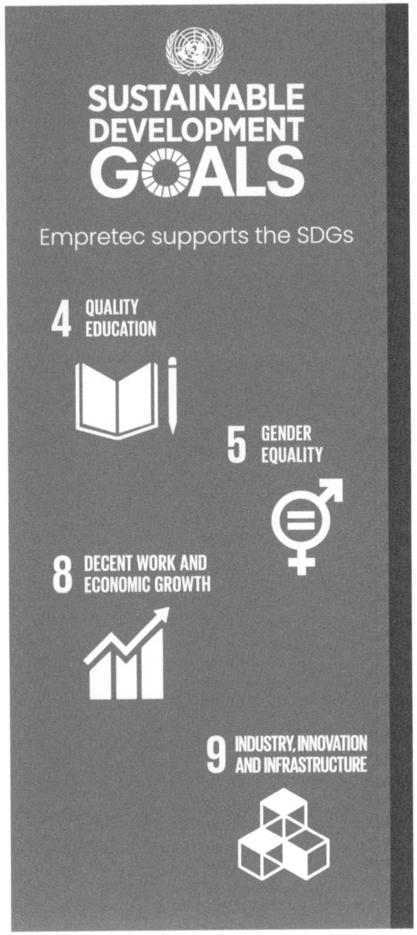

Empretec by the numbers

ESTABLISHED IN 1988

TRAINED HALF A MILLION PEOPLE

7 EMPRETEC WOMEN IN BUSINESS AWARD EVENTS

41 NATIONAL BUSINESS DEVELOPMENT CENTRES AROUND THE WORLD

14,000 ENTREPRENEURSHIP TRAINING WORKSHOPS DELIVERED

1 MILLION PEOPLE ENGAGED BY AWARENESS CAMPAIGNS

FOCUS ON SDGS 4,5,8 & 9

40 INTERNATIONAL MASTER TRAINERS

600 LOCAL CERTIFIED TRAINERS

TRAINING IN 12 LANGUAGES

10 EMPRETEC CORE COMPETENCIES

- Goal-setting
- Information-seeking
- Systematic planning and monitoring
- Opportunity-seeking and initiative
- Persistence
- Fulfilling commitments
- Demand for efficiency and quality
- Taking calculated risks
- Persuasion and networking
- Independence and self-confidence

The Empretec Women in Business awards: Raising awareness, profiling women role-models

The past decade saw little progress on the number of women who own businesses globally. Between 2010 and 2019, globally, 68% of firms did not have any women involved in their ownership. Only 16% of all businesses around the world were owned by women.

The low number of women in business comes at a cost. The economic and social impact associated with women's underrepresentation in business include lower economic growth and less decent employment. Loss of income from women's inactivity can reach up to 30% of gross domestic product in countries with high gender inequality.

To raise awareness on this costly gender gap and to promote women's entrepreneurship, UNCTAD launched the Empretec Women in Business awards in 2008. The awards recognise the contributions of inspiring women entrepreneurs trained by the Empretec programme, to celebrate their success, boost their recognition, and to empower women in general.

The award, granted every two years, has made a real impact on the lives of past recipients. It has improved their access to further training, widened their markets and resources and boosted their motivation to continue growing their enterprises. It has also helped these women become role models in their communities, and beyond.

Recipients excelled in developing innovative business ideas, providing jobs, and increasing incomes in their communities. To date, UNCTAD has received 280 nominations, and awarded 72 finalists from 31 countries over seven editions of the Empretec Women in Business awards. For many, the recognition has been life- and game-changing.

The finalists are selected by a panel of distinguished experts in business and entrepreneurship based on three criteria: innovation, leadership, and impact on their community.

All finalists put their expertise and passion into their businesses, in a variety of sectors, ranging from agri-business to tourism, manufacturing and education.

They have overcome obstacles and persevered to establish and grow successful companies, creating jobs and giving back to their communities, spearheading cultural changes, and serving as role models.

AWARD HISTORY

The UNCTAD Empretec Women in Business Awards have been hosted at different events since they were launched in 2008.

2008
UNCTAD XII Ministerial Conference, Ghana

2010
Annual session of UNCTAD's Investment, Enterprise and Development Commission, Switzerland

2012
UNCTAD XIII and the World Investment Forum, Qatar

2014
World Investment Forum, Switzerland

2016
UNCTAD XIV and the World Investment Forum, Kenya

2018
World Investment Forum, Switzerland

2020
Held online during the COVID-19 pandemic, as a precursor to the 7th World Investment Forum in 2021

Challenging Gender Stereotypes

Women can do anything men can do. But much of the world of work is still parted along gender lines today. Why does this persist?

Research shows that self-confidence for young girls plummets at around the age of 8 and struggles to recover while boys' confidence tends to climb. Little girls need women to look up to ensure they truly believe they can do anything and achieve their dreams.

Still, things are changing, and the situation is improving. The impact of gender policies that favour women, a public and private sector push toward greater parity, and the prominence of women leaders, role models and mentors is creating a more even playing field and inspiring women to step into non-traditional careers in male-dominated industries.

The stories in this section showcase how women are breaking into men's industries and through the glass ceiling. We chat to a female mechanic from Brazil; we engage a security company owner who's shifted the industry in Zimbabwe; we talk with a mother-wife turned social entrepreneur from India; and connect with a construction business founder from Mozambique.

What do they have in common? They're challenging gender stereotypes daily and succeeding.

Femme métale: Ace Brazilian mechanic

It takes a certain mettle to achieve what Agda Óliver has done with her small business. The Brazilian entrepreneur is a magical mechanic hacking it in a man's world by starting the country's first woman-owned car repair service.

It all started with a familiar situation for many women: being scammed by car mechanics. Frustrated by this whenever she took her car in for a service, Agda Óliver went on a mission to find out if other women had the same experience – and to do something about it.

This was 2010. The fear and frustration underlying her experience was real and validated by other women she spoke to. Many shared the same anxiety of not knowing whether the mechanic's diagnostic was real or not; the humiliation of being jeered at for asking basic questions; and the cost of extensive but unnecessary repairs. Sound familiar?

What others accepted as fate, Agda saw as opportunity. Now she's been the owner of Meu Mecânico, a mechanical workshop located in Ceilândia, Brazil, for more than a decade.

The woman-owned and run car repair service employs seven people, most of whom are women from the local community.

In a typically male-dominated profession, Agda is deliberately hiring and training women who share her same passion for cars. This, she says, has created the empathy needed to offer high-quality services to her clients.

"Our biggest challenge was and still is the prejudice against women working in the car repair business. In Brazil, we are the first car repair service for women by women, offering transparent services in a safe and comfortable environment," says Agda.

REVVING MEU MECÃNICO UP

When Agda first consulted her family about starting a car workshop, they were shocked and reluctant to support her. But she was determined. She crafted a business plan, did customer and market research, and explored what it would take to set up and run the shop.

But she still needed help and so enlisted the support of her husband and family, who slowly came around to the idea. "Involve your family and convince them early, so that they can support you in your business," says Agda.

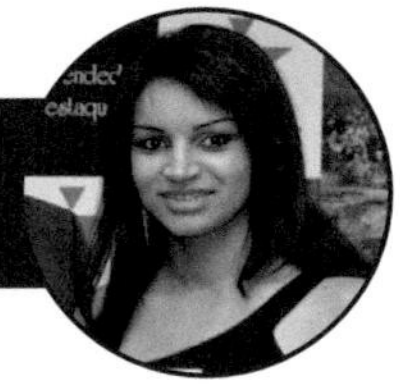

AGDA ÓLIVER
Owner, Meu Mecânico
BRAZIL

Agda had identified the problem. But delivering the solution required more hands on deck and some business guidance.

For this Agda turned to the Brazilian Support Service for Micro and Small Businesses (Sebrae). Sebrae hosts Empretec in Brazil and provides technical and soft skills training, and advisory services to people who plan to start their own business.

With their help, Agda developed a comprehensive business plan which set her on a pathway to success.

The next step was to build a female first workshop and recruit women mechanics. Agda searched across Brazil for women with the technical skills to work in her workshop.

She personally picked each employee and has supported their professional development leading to low staff turnover and happy clients.

"I strive to keep customers satisfied in the long term over profits in the short term," says Agda. "I also organize free lectures and workshops that teach women how to take care of their cars and not be fooled in auto repair shops."

BECOMING AN ENTREPRENEUR

Adga always had an entrepreneurial streak, despite growing up in a traditional family who supported more conventional career paths. When she started the workshop, she was studying computer science. She's since added business management and mechanical engineering degrees to her CV.

But her real entrepreneurial support came from Empretec, she said, which helped her expand her skills, work on strengths and weaknesses, and improve her persuasion powers and ability to delegate.

"When I started, I didn't know how to delegate tasks. I believed I was the only one able to take care of car servicing with quality, but I realized that, on my own, I would not grow. After Empretec, it was so natural to delegate, and that allowed me to have more time to manage my business."

Empretec also helped her understand how to be in tune with the customer. "Here in Brazil, customers expect a little more than what they pay. So, entrepreneurs need to deliver more than expected to establish a strong relationship with your clients," says Agda.

Agda's hard work and business success have been recognized widely. In 2011 and 2012, she was awarded Sebrae's outstanding entrepreneur honour and in 2013 the Brazilian national business woman award. In 2020, Agda was selected as one of the ten finalists the 7th edition of the Empretec Women in Business awards.

Her rise to prominence has inspired other women to pursue less traditional career tracks for women.

Agda says she would like to expand and wants to open Brazil's first mechanics school for women.

FIND OUT MORE

https://www.instagram.com/meumecanicooficial/

Meet Zimbabwe's security industry queen

Divine Ndhlukula was always a dreamer with a penchant for turning dreaming into doing. The result is her hugely successful security company, Securico. It provides security to different industries and is a big cash management player in Zimbabwe.

Divine Ndhlukula is the founder and managing director of an innovative security company in Zimbabwe. Divine's brainchild, Securico, is the southern African nation's first ISO certified security company. It's breaking new ground in both the industry and different spin offs of it.

Securico is also fast becoming the country's biggest player in cash management, supporting with everything from armoured vehicles and high security vaults to safeguarding documents and cash.

But it's also a company that's looking for novel opportunities and new ideas, driven by Divine's entrepreneurial mindset. A prime example is her idea to install solar panels on CCTV cameras and other technology to combat the problem of unreliable power in Zimbabwe.

THE GENESIS OF SECURICO

Divine was always on a mission to solve a problem from early on. Although she didn't always have the technical skills, she had what makes entrepreneurs: vision and passion for a problem.

"I used to dream big as a young girl," she says. "An entrepreneur is someone who sees opportunities and I saw a lot of them. I wasn't going to work for anybody for so long."

The side hustle bug bit early on at her first job at the Zimbabwe Broadcasting Corporation. At work she would find and sell factory reject clothes to her colleagues and friends. But she was on a quest for a bigger breakthrough: a business that was scalable enough to make a change. She saw opportunity in the male-dominated security sector. Although she had no experience, she felt she had a secret sauce.

She saw that the sector's hard edges needed a woman's soft touch. She decided to build her service on two principles: creating more value for customers and improving employee satisfaction.

Divine realized that boosting employees' morale would make them more likely to provide better service which would create happier customers: a virtuous circle.

DIVINE NDHLUKULA
Owner, Securico
ZIMBABWE

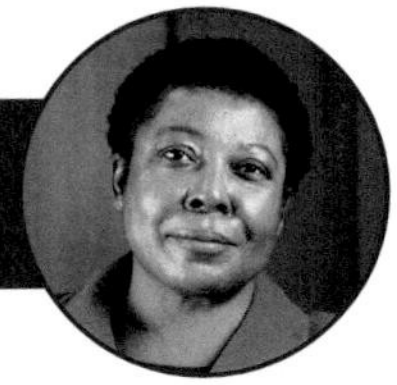

But it took some convincing for customers to accept proposals from this small but mighty woman. "They would look at me from top to bottom," she says. "Being a small person by stature, they would ask: what do you know about security?"

And it wasn't only the customers who didn't back her, the banks also wouldn't provide a loan. "Just because the bank didn't give me money, I couldn't stop my business. So, I sold my house and rented a small house for us to get by."

In just two years her business started growing. "Now I own as many houses as I want to. I had faith in myself. Banks approach to ask if I want a loan. I turn them down."

CHANGING A MAN'S WORLD

Divine's purpose went beyond helping a traditional sectoral transformation. She wanted to help women and create gender parity in the industry. But most customers wanted male security staff. Divine convinced them that there were jobs for women and that women could do the same work as the men.

Even getting women to believe they could do the job was hard. Divine had to really push those who came forward to embrace the opportunity. "I had to literally take them by the hand and say: come on, we can do this. It took conscious and deliberate effort to get it going."

Today women constitute 26% of the workforce in Securico. Most security companies in the country can barely reach a 0.4% women employee rate.

AWARDS WORTH WINNING

Divine was among the top 10 finalists of the UNCTAD's Empretec Women in Business awards in 2014. She attributes much of her success to her family, supportive parents and late husband, her Empretec training and an unfailing self-confidence nurtured early in life.

Divine joined the Empretec training programme in the nineties and it gave her the personal confidence to leave the family business she then headed and go out alone with Securico. This is because of Empretec's focus on boosting her ability to demand efficiency and quality. "It did wonders for our business."

But she says entrepreneurship is not easy. "Success does not happen if you sit at home watching soap operas. There are so many opportunities. Get out, look for opportunities. Read widely. Lastly, networking is important," she advised future entrepreneurs.

Divine has changed the face of the security in Zimbabwe leading BBC World to call her the "queen of the security industry".

FIND OUT MORE

http://securico.co.zw/
https://instagram.com/securicozim
https://www.linkedin.com/in/divine-ndhlukula-70391a19
https://www.facebook.com/divinesimbindhlukula

From social entrepreneurial zero to shero

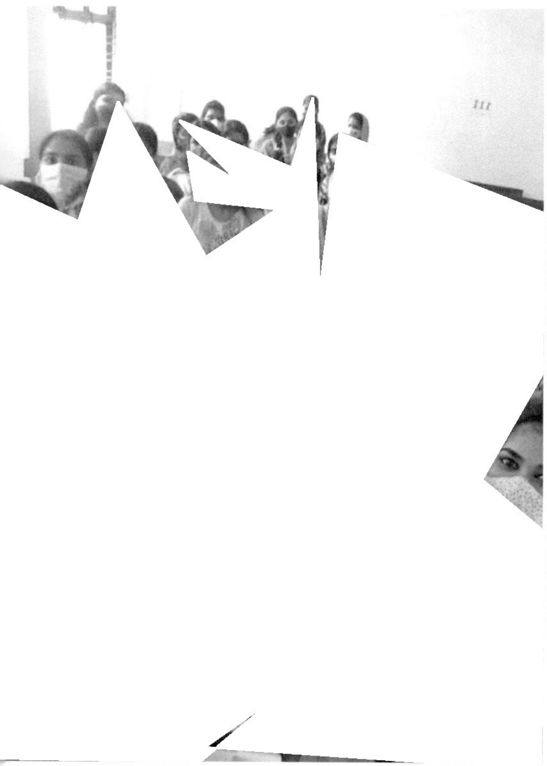

Dr Chandra Vadhana didn't want to atrophy in traditional Indian family life. So, she took her skills and lessons of failure and turned them into a non-profit, Prayaana Labs, that now helps millions of Indian women return to work after a career break.

Gender bias can either cripple your development or catalyse it. This is the lesson that Dr Chandra Vadhana learnt on her own catalytic journey into social entrepreneurship.

As with most transformations, metamorphosis started with a crisis. In Chandra's case, she lacked direction after getting married and becoming a mother. Like many Indian women, settling into married life, raising children was seen as her primary responsibility. But this situation was not enough for Chandra.

Before getting married Chandra was a high performer with a very good job and salary, so she knew what was possible. It took a mindset shift to see her situation more as a career break than the end of the line. During this "break" she enrolled for a part-time course in psychology and set up a home-based recruitment consultancy with a colleague.

"I utilised my career break period for many productive purposes. I studied, attended training, wrote blogs, enrolled in a PhD, worked as an insurance agent, hosted events and did many other menial jobs that were just not a match for my qualifications," she says.

FAILURE AS THE PATH TO ENTREPRENEURSHIP

Her initial recruitment venture failed due to lack of funds, and with it any family support for future businesses. What next, she thought? But failure couldn't keep this extraordinary woman from a small town in Kerala down. She found another job which helped her rebuild her confidence. Then, in 2012, she had a revelation, realising her calling was always entrepreneurship.

So she started another training business, 4TuneFactory, with great ambition. Failure came knocking again. Chandra experienced gender bias in the training field and eventually lost all the money she loaded to start the business.

Not to be deterred, in 2017, she tried again, but this time armed with more knowledge and the arsenal of lessons from the past failures. And so,

CHANDRA VADHANA
Founder of Prayaana Labs
INDIA

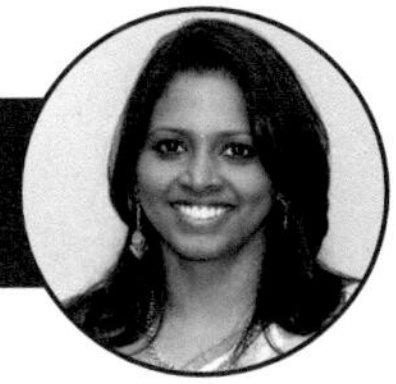

Prayaana Labs was born. The goal? To help women like her, who ended up "redundant" and "valueless" beyond family life.

Prayaana Labs now supports women entrepreneurs with a strong business network and mentorship. It is growing and has expanded to other parts of India, thanks to both technology platforms and a group of Prayaana Ambassadors, spread throughout the country, who work towards the cause of building women's careers.

Chandra aims to touch millions of lives in the coming decade. "I realised that it's my calling to work for the cause of women and fighting gender biases," Chandra says.

THE EMPRETEC DOOR OPENS

In 2016 Chandra attended her first Empretec workshop, sponsored by the local government. She didn't even have the money to travel to Chennai where the workshop was being conducted. She borrowed funds from her cousin to attend. She was the only woman entrepreneur in that cohort. The moment was "life-changing", she says.

The Empretec training convinced her not to give up. And she didn't. Today she successfully runs multiple ventures under the Prayaana Collective banner which is a 100% women-owned enterprise, employing more than 100 women directly and indirectly.

These include Pracol.com, India's first women empowerment e-commerce platform, SheSight magazine, a digital magazine featuring global women achievers, and the Peaks Academy, an e-learning platform.

Chandra went on to win a 2018 Empretec Women in Business award, the only Indian in the social enterprise category to do so to date. "The confidence boost which came with the award and the competencies gained is immense," she says.

"Personal entrepreneurial competencies help not just in business but also in all walks of life." After being part of Empretec she not only scaled her business but also completed her long-pending PhD.

Chandra now wants to empower one million women through employability and entrepreneurship initiatives by 2030. She emphasizes that this goal propels all her business and personal decisions.

According to Chandra, women possess immense potential to make a positive impact in the world, but only if they embrace a mindset of possibility.

"As an entrepreneur, it's also our responsibility to the next generation to contribute our potential. So, go, do your best. Never settle for less," she says.

Chandra turned her challenges and failures into the stepping stones to her success, battling gender bias and relentlessly working to empower women.

FIND OUT MORE

https://www.instagram.com/dr.ceevee/
https://twitter.com/cvadhana
https://www.linkedin.com/in/connectceevee/
https://www.facebook.com/dr.ceevee/

Breaking civil engineering stereotypes

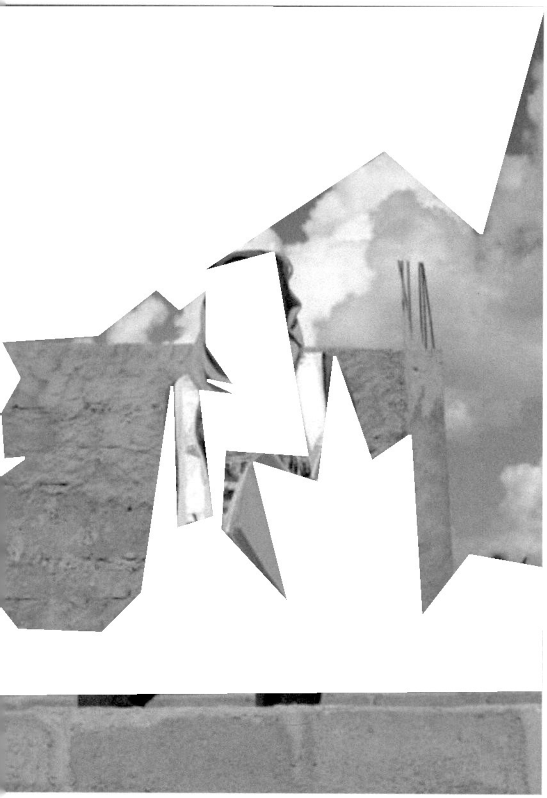

When Uneiza Ali Issufo started ConsMoz Limited she knew she would be breaking ground of a different sort as she reached to challenge the male-dominated construction industry. Little did she know how far she would go.

Mozambican construction whizz Uneiza Ali Issufo has always been a little audacious and persistent, character traits that led her to become a frontrunner in the country's construction industry.

Initially Uneiza wanted to study architecture, but her father persuaded her to try civil engineering. Even though she knew little about it, she took his advice, thinking it was a good idea to challenge a male-dominated field in a positive way. The rest is history. Now ConsMoz is a massive player in Mozambique's construction sector.

Buoyed by the benefits of Empretec training Uneiza, also an MBA (Master of Business Administration) graduate, was able to expand her business to employ 800 people and land large building contracts with a focus on sustainability.

HOW IT STARTED, HOW IT'S GOING

Starting a construction business was not easy. The main reason was trust, she says. "Or more accurately, a lack thereof." As a young woman in a man's world, Uneiza had to start all jobs trying to convince people, and even her own team, of her capabilities.

Luckily, tackling hurdles was not a big deal for her. She had tremendous support from her parents who always supported her curious side.

"Once, I wanted to learn to change the flat tire of my car, or pour water in the radiator, they would help me learn how. They allowed me to pursue my curiosity," she says. This created a daughter who would never give up – a trait that's carried over to her business. So, when a multi-national company was commissioned to do construction work in Mozambique, Uneiza, persistently requested an opportunity from them. Eventually she was offered the chance to build 10 houses – but was initially overwhelmed by the job.

As luck would have it, she met a businessman whilst flying back from a meeting who was interested in her project and work. He said he wanted to "pay it forward" and help someone in their early career, and promised Uneiza a truck, a driver, and some capital to kickstart the build.

UNEIZA ALI ISSUFO
Founding member, ConsMoz Limited
MOZAMBIQUE

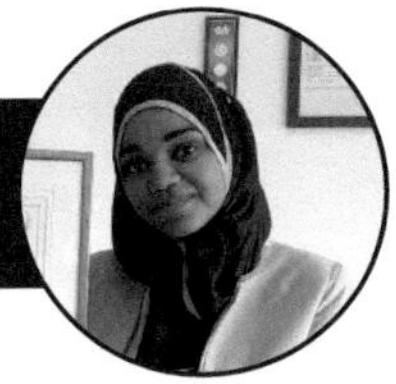

This proved to be a major turning point in her life and the construction went ahead. After two weeks, an engineer came to inspect her work. He was surprised to see how well she had done. She was quickly assigned another 40 houses. Then the target increased from 40 to 400 a week later.

However, Uneiza didn't have the resources to make such a leap. The labour and raw materials alone to build the 400 houses was a massive financial stretch.

Somehow, she negotiated the procurement of the materials on credit and finished the job. This is indicative of a work ethic and tenacity that has guided her company to growth.

A CULTURE OF TEAMWORK

From early on Uneiza realized that the work was more than just about building homes, it was about managing teams to deliver. Underpinning this approach was a competency she learned during Empretec training: the demand for quality and efficiency.

Applying this learning led to the creation of a fun culture of teamwork amid her labourers – by introducing some healthy competition.

How? She came up with the brilliant idea of dividing her labourers into four competing teams. Each one would represent a country in a FIFA-type tournament.

The best employee would get their name and picture printed on a T-shirt, and all other employees would wear that same t-shirt, creating a "football star".

The workers loved being the best player and the concept and culture took off. Since then, she's continued to organize similar competitions to meet the deadlines more efficiently.

ALL CREDIT TO EMPRETEC

Initially, Uneiza was reluctant to attend the Empretec workshop as she thought it would distract her from her company and she was already overcommitted in several industry leadership roles. But her profile made her a good fit; and she was invited by her city mayor to join the local Empretec chapter.

She says Empretec was an interesting program. "I already had several aptitudes," she said. "But Empretec helped me consolidate certain characteristics that had a positive impact on my enterprise and on the way I behaved."

The hard work paid off and she won gold at the 2018 Empretec Women in Business awards. Uneiza now mentors young girls. "If you want to change the world, you have to change yourself first to inspire other people," she says.

FIND OUT MORE

https://www.instagram.com/uneizaali/
https://www.facebook.com/uneiza.aliissufo
https://www.linkedin.com/in/uneiza-issufo-1536794b/

Family Support:

The Key to Success

Having your family back you when you go into business can and does help launch and sustain enterprises, but even more so when that help is in support of women entrepreneurs. Without this kind of support, entrepreneurs have a much harder time achieving success.

Today, UNCTAD research shows two-thirds of businesses worldwide are owned or managed by families, employing 60% of the world's workforce and contributing over 70% of global GDP.

The key to success, really does lie in family support – whether they are just behind you when you start out or get involved in creating a business.

UNCTAD knows the power of strong family backing for business and our Empretec programme is flush with stories where families are the reason for the continued success of enterprises, especially those started and run by women.

In this section, we hear some of those voices – women who are succeeding because their families encourage them to continue and grow.

We connect with an Argentine woman who wants to put a stop to single use plastics, by creating cutlery made from cane reeds, and who couldn't do so without her family's help.

We tap into the vision of an Ecuadorian eco-farmer and chef who is driving rural tourism with an eco-edge on her family farm. And we explore the story of a Ugandan social entrepreneur and "pumpkin queen" who uses each part of the pumpkin to produce everything from juice to oil, all for the benefit of rural women and their children.

Putting a fork in single-use plastics

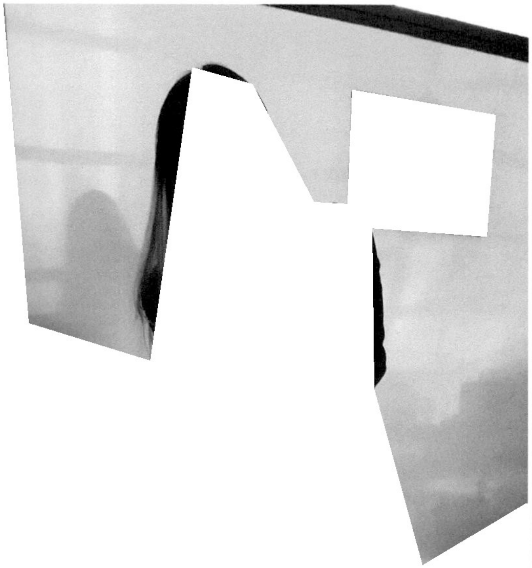

Plastic pollution in Argentina is no match for Paula Itatí De la Vega Sánchez who, after witnessing a fire in a cane field, saw an opportunity that led her to a bold and innovative idea: biodegradable cutlery made from the giant reeds.

Argentine Paula Itatí De la Vega Sánchez wanted to eat healthy as an agricultural engineering student but had very little money to do so. When she returned home to the countryside after university, she decided she wanted to grow her own organic vegetables to keep healthy.

The mission was going well until it came time to irrigate the plot. She discovered that the irrigation channels were full of garbage, especially disposable plastics. This is when she realised the extent to which the world is reliant on plastic products.

Always entrepreneurial, Paula started making salads from her vegetable garden. She would sell the bowls to office workers at affordable prices, as a healthy meal option.

One day a customer asked her for utensils with the meal. She knew she didn't want to use plastic. So she set out to look for green options, which turned out to be expensive and difficult to find. Eureka – an opportunity, she thought.

This, coupled with a fire incident in the local cane fields, generated an ah ha! moment for Paula who saw potential in making cutlery from the remnants of the plants. The result is her company Bioita Ecubiertos, which makes biodegradable cane utensils and straws out of giant reeds.

A FORK IN THE ROAD

Her first attempt was not a success. She found a partner, and they invested in developing initial cane cutlery products. Unfortunately, the partnership did not end well. At that time, Paula was expecting a baby and was preparing for life as a single mom. She had also lost the government subsidy she had secured for the business.

"When you hit rock bottom, there is no choice but to get up," she says. And that is what she did. With financial assistance from her father, she purchased the required tools, paid for the design of a brand, a photographer, and bought carpentry supplies. She started making cutlery by hand. She sold them in stores, at exhibitions, and offered them to everyone in the business of sustainability.

PAULA ITATÍ DE LA VEGA SÁNCHEZ
Chief executive, Bioita Ecubiertos
ARGENTINA

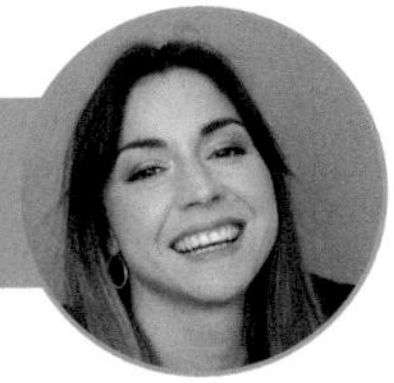

Slowly and steadily, she managed to expand her product distribution and scale up her business.

Paula overcame many challenges in handcrafting her cutlery, but this was complimented with several lucky breaks. She accessed a seed-funding grant from Argentina's Ministry of Productive Development. With that money, she bought her first industrial machine.

> **"Never be afraid to take up risks or feel more confident about yourselves to take the step forward in life."**

But the machinery was tricky to operate and her initial attempts did not succeed. Paula got frustrated.

A friend she met while attending Empretec training in 2018 intervened. Her friend encouraged her to embrace a resilience mindset, urging Paula not to give up. Paula cleared her mind and focused on finding a solution. Eventually she found a new processing method for the machine.

This paved the way towards manufacturing the cutlery products successfully. Now she's planning to expand to other countries.

A PRO-WOMEN, FOR NATURE WORK ENVIRONMENT

Paula says that the conflicts she experienced in her personal and professional life have made her contemplate the lives and careers of women.

While the business focuses on sustainability, it also pays close attention to creating an equal and a positive work environment for women employees.

She decided to fix on hiring mainly single mothers. She offered them a four-hour work day policy to ensure they have time to study, do other activities or dedicate time to their children.

She also wants to promote plant biodiversity in rural areas because she feels that global warming is negatively affecting the soils. Cane, she thinks, is part of the solution. Right now, she is working in a way to optimize the production of her cutlery to reduce the company's carbon footprint. And she now plans to spread her cane business to Africa and support women by promoting the four-hour work shift.

Paula is determined to achieve her objectives. Her work won her the Empretec Women in Business award 2020 accolade in the Circular Economy category.

"As a single woman or a mother, never be afraid to take up risks or feel more confident about yourselves to take the step forward in life," she advises women entrepreneurs.

"Women have strong will power, so make use of the skills in you and just race ahead in whichever career you choose. Uncertainty lasts forever in life. So use your skills and ideas to the best of your ability."

FIND OUT MORE

https://bioita.com.ar/
https://www.youtube.com/channel/UCyx_ZUgOjzN7g9fiG_AKNcw
https://www.linkedin.com/in/paula-itat%C3%AD-de-la-vega-sánchez-144aba16a/
https://www.facebook.com/pidlavs/

Family farming with an eco-bent

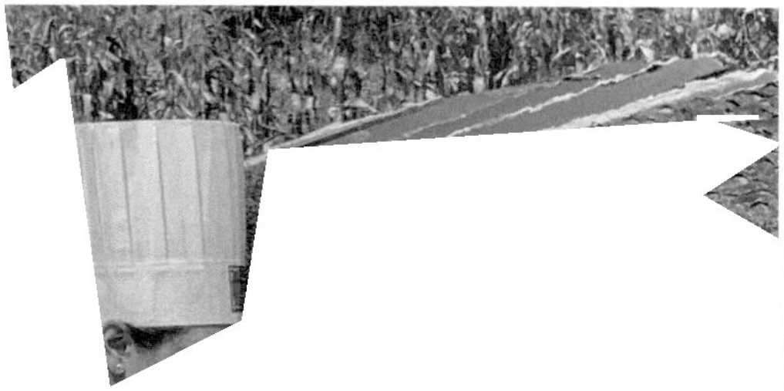

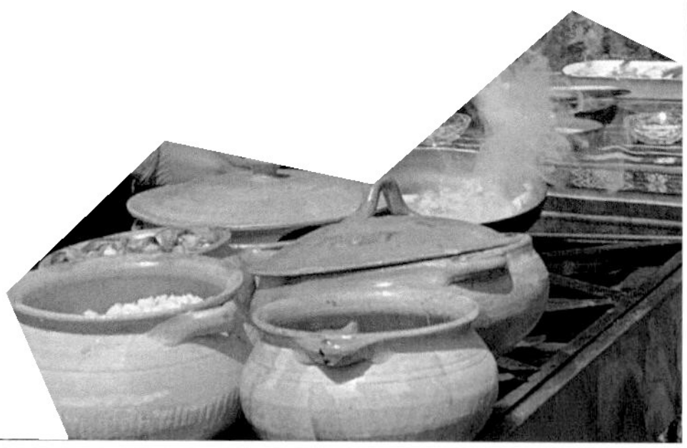

Ana María Villavicencio Flores from Ecuador doesn't like chemicals on her plants and believes neither should other people. Her company and farm Finca Agroturistica Don Antonio have embraced a chemical-free method that inspires guests to take environmental action.

Ana María Villavicencio is an enthusiastic pioneer of environmentally friendly farming practices and agri-tourism in Ecuador. Her sustainable farm, Finca Don Antonio, specializes in harvesting chemical-free products that offer natural experiences to tourists such as horseback riding and food tastings.

Ana María provides an eco-escape and in so doing is driving rural tourism. The enterprise is a family affair. The farm – home to an agri-ecological orchard, vast land where farm animals are reared, and a restaurant in the family house – also offers space for local artisans to display and sell their products; and Ana María is the chef at the restaurant.

Ana María credits her parents for her journey. Proximity to nature and the high potential in farming drove Ana María and her siblings to pick academic pathways that would transform the family farm into a family business. Her brothers studied veterinary science and agronomy, and she became an industrial agricultural engineer and chef.

CATALYTIC CUSTOMER FEEDBACK

In 2018, a visitor to the farm suggested they create a space that's open for tourists who may want to have the experience of being on an ecological farm.

Inspired by what he saw, this customer connected the family with the Ecuadorian Ministry of Tourism. As luck would have it, the introduction came at an opportune time. The ministry had just opened a contest for entrepreneurs in the tourism sector.

Ana María registered the business idea. From around 468 contestants, Ana won the award. This made her realise their potential in the agri-tourism industry and gave them the impetus to start Finca Agroturistica Don Antonio.

A FARM TO TABLE EXPERIENCE

When visitors arrive to the farm they receive a warm welcome with a refreshing drink, and are taken on a tour of the orchard. On the tour

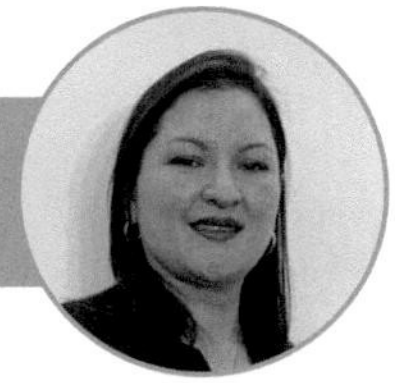

ANA MARÍA VILLAVICENCIO FLORES
Owner, Finca Agroturistica Don Antonio
ECUADOR

the family explains the different techniques they use to grow food.

The experience includes visiting and feeding the animals and a horseback tour. It closes with a world class organic culinary experience offering a menu of the traditional local cuisine with a gourmet twist – all served up by Ana María.

> **"I was guided on the best techniques and processes to crystalize the actual enterprise in real life."**

Puchero – soup made with pork backbone and vegetables – is one of the typical dishes served at the farm's restaurant. Dessert is an Ana María creation: goldenberry mousse. But it has not all been easy.

A COVID-19 PIVOT

In 2020, COVID-19 put all tourism to Ecuador on hold. Ana María took action during this time and started diversifying the farm's services.

In May 2020, Mothers' Day celebrations were approaching. So she decided to bring the farm's culinary experience to people's homes alongside a special serenade to lift spirits. This birthed the farm's special catering packages, which Ana María promoted on social media.

The response was significant. During COVID-19 the family also realised that the farm was completely self-sustainable; and could even sell surplus food produce and share it with neighbours.

The pandemic helped the business become more resilient. In part this is due to competencies that Ana María learned at a 2018 Empretec workshop.

AN EXPANSION ORIENTATION

"The Empretec experience was very enriching. I was guided on the best techniques and processes to crystalise the actual enterprise in real life," says Ana María.

"It taught me to see the opportunities, strengthen my support networks, focus on each step and systematise them so that it all could be put in practice after the workshop," she says. A valuable learning for her was "to learn by doing". She is now applying this approach with the guests, who come to the farm and learn how to make marmalade and other products.

"The most important skills I developed out of Empretec training are having a clear vision, setting appropriate goals, planning, and using ideas in a systematic way."

Ana María was awarded the Special Prize for Entrepreneurship in Sustainable Agriculture at the 2020 edition of the Empretec Women in Business awards. She now has plans to build other facilities to expand the services. For instance, to move the restaurant from the family home into a proper facility.

Additionally, tourists often ask for lodging, so she plans offering accommodation. Her next goals are to provide better premium services, employ more local people and boost the local economy.

FIND OUT MORE

https://www.instagram.com/fincadonantonio/
https://www.facebook.com/fincadonantonio.ec

The power of a simple pumpkin patch

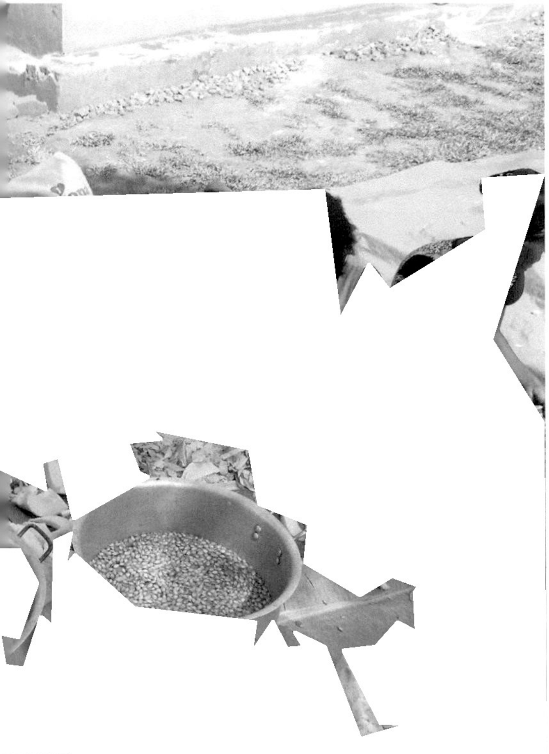

Joyce Kyalema's chariot for helping rural women increase their household income and food security comes in the form of a pumpkin. Her pumpkin kingdom employs over 50 women, forging a one-of-a-kind, sustainable agribusiness in Uganda.

Joyce Kyalema started JOSMAK International (U) Limited in 2014 on a mission to put the pumpkin, a simple and easily grown but underutilised vegetable, on the map. Her business now helps alleviate child malnutrition and reduce unemployment among young women, while promoting sustainability.

All this from the idea bank of secretary turned social entrepreneur. While working as a secretary at her father's firm, the duo frequently visited their village where she observed fields of pumpkins grown by local women. The crop was mostly for home consumption, with the rest sold cheaply, and the balance going to animal feed.

Joyce saw an opportunity in the excess produce and all the by-products going to waste. Now JOSMAK salvages and transforms the entire pumpkin from pips to pulp into viable products.

FROM SEED TO SALE

Pumpkin seeds are nutritious but difficult to chew through. Joyce realised you can make flour from the seeds to make cakes, cookies and snacks like bagia, a popular snack in Uganda.

Since she didn't have any machines, she rallied the rural women farmer she collaborated with to get their own mortars; they pounded the dried pumpkin and pumpkin seeds separately, creating two different types of powders, which they sold.

In the process, they used to throw away a lot of fresh pumpkin pulp, so Joyce decided to add value here, too, making juice from it. But the sales of the pumpkin juice were not going as well as expected. People did not like the smell of the pumpkin, so the team experimented. They decided to ferment the juice, and with the addition of other ingredients, the sales of this delicious drink rose.

Now she has four pumpkin products that are in high demand: juice, flour, seeds, and seed flour. As the company grew and experimented, the by-products expanded. The residue generated during sieving and roasting has been re-purposed into tea spice. And any residue is converted into

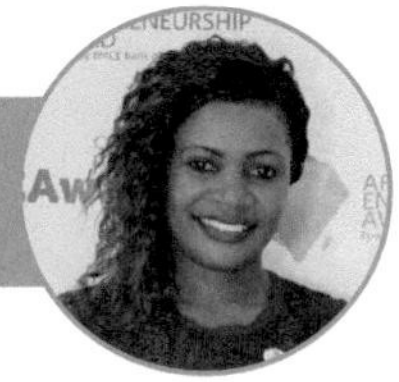

JOYCE KYALEMA
Founder & MD, JOSMAK International (U) Ltd.
UGANDA

animal feed and organic manure for the pumpkin crop.

The team also created pumpkin seed butter, pumpkin oil, pumpkin soup, and pumpkin leaf powder. From one single vegetable, Joyce built a successful business, creating such a diverse range of products, while upholding standards of circularity and sustainable production.

> **"When you network you get ideas, connections and find good people who are willing to help you on the way."**

Today JOSMAK sells to supermarkets, traders, restaurants, hotels, schools and hospitals. Joyce says her success is defined by her passion. "Passion is number one. When you have passion for what you are doing, even if you get stuck on the way, you keep moving. Money shouldn't be your priority, but something else which pushes you towards that business idea."

EDUCATION IS AN ENTRANCE

Her determination to make the lives of youth and women easier is the driving force behind her venture, and the bedrock of JOSMAK's success as a social enterprise. But it started with education.

Joyce received the gift of education from her father in a country where girl-children are not often sent to school. This education gave her a powerful network, something she wants to transmit to other women and girls.

"When you network you get ideas, connections and find good people who are willing to help you on the way," she says.

She was lucky to have her parents' support throughout her entrepreneurial journey. And the more she helps young people and women, the more she reaps the fruits – or vegetables – of her work.

A MATTER OF SCALE

Growing a business is a daily challenge, she says. From procuring and using machinery to moving stock and product. Still, her self-belief and passion propelled her forward despite the challenges.

Her company currently has five separate entities employing over 50 women, forging one-of-a-kind, highly sustainable agribusiness in Uganda.

Currently she is exporting to Kenya and Tanzania through public transit systems. She is also supplying to a store in Boston, in the USA, which sells Ugandan products. She wants JOSMAK to become the leading supplier of pumpkin products worldwide by the year 2025.

Her long list of accolades speaks for themselves and include her being one of 6 finalists in the 2016 Empretec Women in Business award.

Joyce's Empretec experience and award changed people's perspective about her, she said, opening doors for more funding and support to grow her business.

FIND OUT MORE

https://twitter.com/joycekyalema
https://www.linkedin.com/in/joycekyalema/
https://www.facebook.com/joyce.kyalemamichelle

Scaling from a Small to a Medium or Large-sized Company

They say small is beautiful, but big is impactful. Two entrepreneurs from two of Empretec's chapters are leading examples of how something small can scale over time, incrementally and consistently, taking a large group of employees and people with them. As they scale, they make an abiding community and economic impact.

Small and medium-sized enterprises (SMEs) are the axel on which many economies spin, particularly in developing countries. They make up much of all enterprises (90%) globally, and account for most job creation and employment worldwide (50%). The World Bank finds that formal SMEs contribute up to 40% of national income (GDP) in emerging economies. Include the informal outfits, and this number skyrockets, alongside impact.

The journey to scaling a small or medium-sized business into a large one is increasingly important as the world seeks to create another 600 million jobs by 2030 to absorb the growing global workforce. It is thus crucial to explore cases where small businesses have grown considerably, to understand their methods and move to support similar businesses.

In this section we meet two women entrepreneurs who have spent more than 25 years building their businesses. The owner of Uganda's fruit juice empire is already a major player in the East African region and is now foraying into farming and mass production after gaining access to a massive government grant. Then Brazil's lingerie production hub in the southeast of the country owes its growth to the woman who started the movement in 1994 with just a seamstress by her side. Both employ hundreds of people, and indirectly impact thousands.

They are now in the legacy-building dimension of their business lives, and so are equally focused on both company expansion and social impact.

A very juicy story from Mama Cheers

Julian Omalla, better known as "Mama Cheers", makes one of Uganda's most popular fruit juice drinks. But she is also one of the country's leading entrepreneurs, exporters and inspirations for future businesspeople, especially women.

Her story is remarkable. When she started Delight in 1996, she had no idea just how far her business idea would go. She beat cultural bias, and the lack of education, family and financial support, and powerful competitors, to not only scale, but to command almost 45% of the Ugandan drinks market. All with a smile on her face, sowing the delight and positivity on which she built her brand.

Not only has she overcome business challenges, she ultimately won the support of her family, community and government to become one of the leading examples of entrepreneurship. She's also gone about it in the most inclusive way, to ensure her employees benefit and share in the profits and experience, and grow with the company.

She has mobilised and engaged hundreds of vulnerable female farmers ensuring that each woman would have at least one acre of fruit orchard intercropped with short-term seasonal crops for income and sustainability.

In 2021, her work won her more government support. Uganda granted her a $10 million loan to build a fresh juice factory in the north of the country. Her processing line produces 12,000 litres of fruit-flavoured drinks per day. "An entrepreneur should also know that there are all types of weather, some good, some bad. They need to plan ahead of time. Support others and never close their hands," Julian said.

Julian Omalla is chief executive of Uganda's favourite juice maker, Delight Ltd., which produces the popular fruit drink, Cheers. She employs over 1,000 people and exports to Kenya, Rwanda, Sudan and Tanzania.

JUICE TO GET GOING

Julian did not have an easy or clear pathway to entrepreneurship. Ugandan culture doesn't prioritise the education of women and the expectation is that women work to support their families.

She worked many odd jobs in her early life, from operating a small retail shop, to harvesting the fields of her male family members. But her penchant for innovation was always evident. When the farm she was

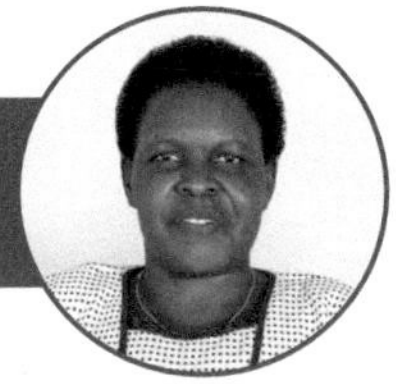

JULIAN ADYERI OMALLA
Founder, CEO of Delight Uganda Ltd.
UGANDA

managing couldn't pay its workers, she found a way to compensate the employees by making refreshments from the bananas harvested on the farm.

She also recognised opportunity, identifying the potential in planting cassava, a popular cash crop, on her brother's farm. But her goal was greater than to work for someone else. She wanted to start her own business.

It took some convincing and the support of a reluctant but ultimately convincible husband. And so Delight and the fruit juice brand, "Cheers" was launched.

Raising funds to expand her business was an uphill task, as she, like most women in Uganda, didn't have the collateral that banks needed to finance her venture. She had to rely on her savings and invest her profits back into the business to finance its expansion.

Competitors and wholesalers also blocked her ascent. Some wholesalers refused to sell her the raw materials needed for production and competitors made it hard for her to survive, but she used each setback as a lesson. "I always learn from setbacks and failures. I never let them put me down," she says.

QUALITY MEANS BUSINESS

Her tenacity and eye for opportunity, backed by a long term relationship with and training from Empretec, enabled her to grow Delight and deliver quality first to her customers.

Until 2011, Julian produced Cheers based on imported juice concentrates, partly due to the challenge of sourcing high-quality and locally grown fresh fruits.

But after she bought a 1700-acre farm in North Uganda for cultivating fruit trees, such as mangoes, guavas and citruses, she was able to guarantee quality while also empowering her employees. "If anyone wants to compete with me on quality," she says, "it would take them a good six years to get there."

Her approach is also inclusive. She established a nursery seed bed to propagate clean fruit planting materials and organised under a cooperative an orchard with 5,000 contracted fruit farmers in the northern district of Nwoya. Of its 5,000 members, the Nwoya Fruit Growers Cooperative has 3,750 women growing fruits for Delight Uganda, benefiting over 100,000 women directly and indirectly.

Julian has also diversified into other business activities, such as poultry farming, maize-feed production, a flour mill and a bakery. She credits Empretec for many of her skills. "The training helped me realize that I was born an entrepreneur," she recalls. "It helped me develop and execute my business growth plan."

She says Empretec improved her self-confidence and other competencies such as goal setting, bookkeeping, marketing, setting targets and working efficiently to meet them. In 2020, Julian won the special award for "Women Empowering Women through Inclusive Business" at the Empretec Women in Business awards.

FIND OUT MORE

http://delightug.com/index.php

Stitching up social innovation

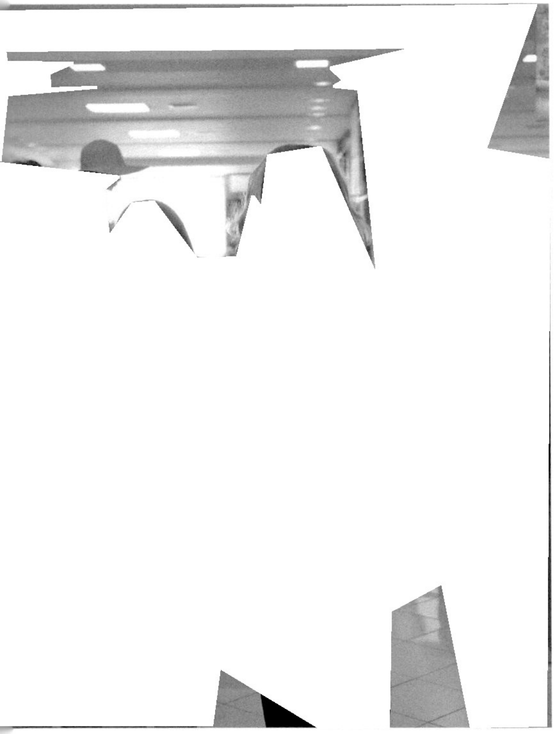

Rosana Marques is working to leave a lingerie legacy in her hometown of Juruaia in Minas Gerais, a state in the southeast region of Brazil. Rosana was instrumental in building the foundations for the undergarment production hub which created the "Capital da Lingerie".

The lingerie company Ouseuse started out small in 1994, with one seamstress and an owner with a vision for creating quality, beautiful, comfortable underwear. Fast forward to 2022, and the company led by Rosana Marques has grown exponentially, putting the town of Juruaia on the map, while birthing a design hub, and bringing new economic hope.

Juruaia in Minas Gerais, is a quiet city with just over ten thousand inhabitants, set in a beautiful natural landscape, it is the perfect location for the lingerie capital it would become, due in large part to the entrepreneurial efforts of Rosana.

Today, Ouseuse employs about 80 people directly and 120 indirectly. Tens of companies have come to establish themselves in Juruaia, driving national lingerie trends while offering well-priced garments and distinctive design and quality.

AN IMPECCABLE METHOD

Rosana wanted to build a company that served the community and created new economic opportunities. She was also concerned for women's health and well-being. This inspired an amazing invention, says Rosana: a line of underwear lined with copper ions, capable of killing up to 99% of the pathogenic microorganisms (such as fungi and bacteria) which cause several types of infections.

It didn't stop there. Well-being is at the core of her ambition. Some of the collections, for example, use insect-repelling fabrics or biodegradable nylon with UV50+ solar protection factor for the fitness lines. While unique, the products are also fashionable, making them very attractive and sought after both in Brazil and abroad.

Rosana mixes being on-trend with the best technologies available, a "powerful combination" she says. For Rosana, her inspiration comes from a need and desire for women in general to wear exquisite lingerie, look alluring and feel confident in their own skin.

"Ouseuse is a tool to empower women," says Rosana. It does so for both the customer and the salesperson. Ouseuse uses a business model that

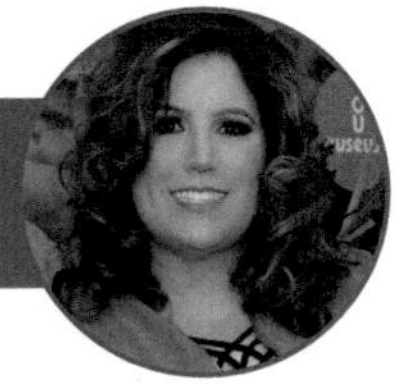

ROSANA MARQUES
Owner of Ouseuse
BRAZIL

enables its women-led sales team to build their work and sales hours around their schedules.

Women can sell the garments in their own time without losing their current jobs or taking time away from their family responsibilities.

GOING OVER AND BEYOND

Rosana's mission to help women didn't stop at the underwear revolution. It expanded to cancer awareness and prevention, fashion upcycling and recycling, and training underprivileged workers.

For example, she launched "Amigas do Peito" or 'bosom friends' in Portuguese, a social project to prevent breast cancer and restore the self-esteem of women who have had a mastectomy.

Similarly, Amiga Recicla collects undergarments which are still in good condition but no longer used. They're recycled through a careful sanitization process and donated to communities in need.

Much of her entrepreneurial and socially minded slant comes from her time being trained by Empretec. The training provided her with the most important tools such as learning to set goals, to plan, calculate risks, choose the right people, train them and place them in the right positions.

She still flows these approaches through her business and social enterprises today, even though Rosana is now a grandmother and focused on family as much as business growth. "I love what I do, not only because I created it, but because I am proud of what I have achieved: making women feel beautiful, attractive and fulfilled," she says.

She is always striving to improve the relationship channels between her customers and sales force. For her, the relationship with customers is the core value of her company. She is constantly investing in technology and tools for understanding consumer behavior in the target markets.

This has ensured Ouseuse's top spot in the underwear industry and it is currently expanding to other countries, including India.

With all that she has accomplished, she believes she has set a path for other entrepreneurs to follow: a lingerie legacy of sorts. "It's giving back what you've earned through good deeds," she says.

Rosana has been recognised for her longstanding achievements. In 2013 she was nominated for the 2013 Claudia Award. She is the first president of the Commerce Association in Juruaia, founder of the Câmara da Mulher Empreendedora (Chamber of Women Entrepreneurs) and is also part of the Women of Brazil project.

In 2018 she was a finalist in the UNCTAD Empretec Women in Business awards.

FIND OUT MORE

https://www.instagram.com/rosanamarquesouseuse/
https://www.facebook.com/rosana.marques.1048

Personal Entrepreneurial Competencies

Since Empretec first launched its training workshop in 1988, more than half a million people have been trained. Many of the trainees have been women. They have benefited greatly from the workshop, which has allowed them to launch or scale their businesses, or even veer in new directions.

The Entrepreneurship Training Workshop uses a methodology of behavioural change that helps entrepreneurs put their ideas into action and aids fledgling businesses to grow. It is a unique, competencies and behavioural-based approach to developing successful entrepreneurs. It changes mindsets, and enhances the productive capacity and international competitiveness of MSMEs. The workshop focuses on helping entrepreneurs gain ground across 10 key personal entrepreneurial competencies.

1. Goal setting
2. Information seeking
3. Systematic planning and monitoring
4. Opportunity seeking and initiative
5. Persistence
6. Fulfilling commitments
7. Demand for efficiency and quality
8. Taking calculated risks
9. Persuasion and networking
10. Independence and self-confidence

In this section we hear from five women whose approach to business was totally transformed by the Empretec training. They applied the newly learned competencies to their everyday business practices, and witnessed the results.

We hear from a Zambian woman tackling food security through her multi-product shop; a Guyana-based creator bringing joy at her retreat; a Jordanian tech-trainer helping young people get future-proofed; and another Jordanian chocoholic reshaping the sweet industry.

We go on to meet an El Salvadorian on a mission to recycle and upcycle waste; and a Panama-based chef protecting local culinary traditions and advocating for food as medicine.

A big bite of business

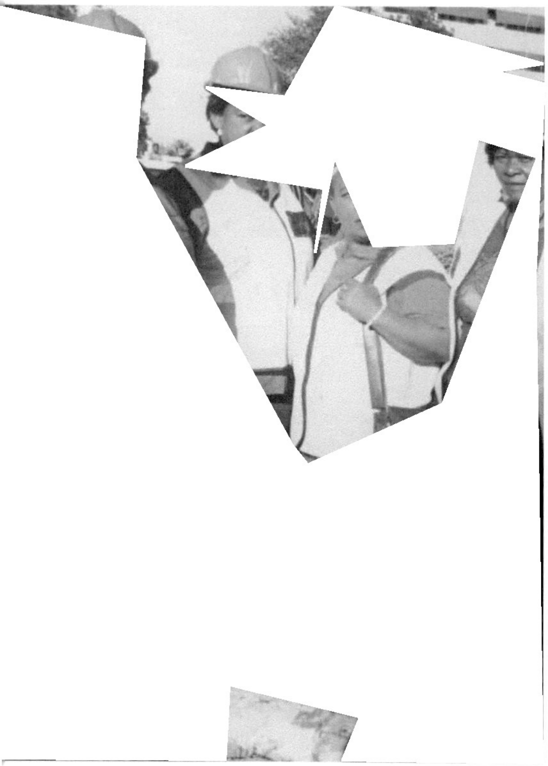

Angelica Magdallen Rumsey took people's love of food and desire for ease and turned a takeaway delivery business into a multi-product shop. In the process she's helped Zambian women ensure their own food security and income generation.

Zambia is not always a country where women's development and education is prioritised. But when families do so, the results can be phenomenal, as is the case with Angelica Magdallen Rumsey.

Angelica is a food entrepreneur with a passion for being a social and political reformer. Her company, Angel Bites Limited, is the result of years of work, underpinned by the education and support she received from her family. She also runs the Shiwangandu Development Trust, an NGO founded in 2005, which works with vulnerable groups of women and youth.

Her father and grandfather were both successful businessmen in northern Zambia. And her mother ran the household like a business too, says Angelica. This exposure turned Angelica into an entrepreneur herself.

When she failed to qualify for university entrance, she decided to do a secretarial course to help get her a job. She worked for a few prominent institutions including the International Labour Organization, but she often dreamt of creating greater impact and her own business.

UNDERSTANDING FOOD SECURITY

In Zambia, most people rely on agriculture to make a living, especially women who traditionally have less access to productive resources, services and opportunities, including land, financial services and education.

Angelica witnessed this first hand when growing up. She was raised in a rural area with few facilities. The family used to grow most of their own food, selling the excess off when needed. This gave Angelica a special insight into the necessity of food security, so when she parted ways with her siblings on a clothing, hardware, and household shop they had opened, food was her logical entrepreneurial starting point.

Angel Bites started selling locally produced food from a bespoke menu. Angelica started selling takeaway meals and eventually opened a shop where she sold groceries, bakery, and butchery products. She involved local producers and women from the outset. Angel Bites works actively with an "out-grower model".

ANGELICA MAGDALLEN RUMSEY
Owner of Angel Bites Limited
ZAMBIA

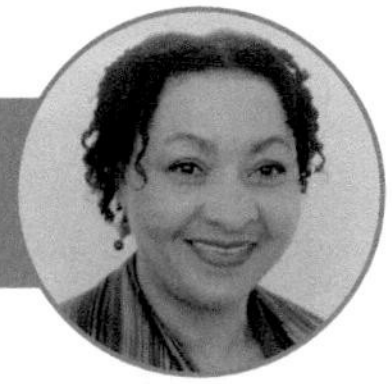

This approach focuses on producers who grow and supply products on account of nutritional value. These products are organically grown and area-specific. Examples include sorghum, millet, cassava, maize, beans, groundnuts, dried vegetables, as well as dried fish (kapenta and breams), and dried caterpillars (finkubala).

A GENDER LENS

Angelica's entrepreneurial journey was not smooth. Gender bias played a role in some of the obstacles she encountered.

"Especially in the business world, when you try to compete with men to get tenders or orders from certain institutions there is a certain tendency to favour men over women. When you encounter a male competitor, they try to pull down their female counterpart," she muses.

"Oftentimes, men feel insecure with a woman's success, so they try to put obstacles in her way in every possible manner. In rural areas, traditionally, men are the head of a house and make decisions for the family. It is the men who always get titles for land, but a woman is never given this right of ownership."

Angelica believes that she should not keep to herself what she knows but share with others. She also believes that if women work together, sharing the knowledge they have, they can raise their communities and nations in such a way that "men will have no choice but to listen to us."

Angelica's mission is to help as many women as possible, to uplift and empower them spiritually, emotionally, and economically.

AWARDED FOR EXCELLENCE

In 2014, Angelica made the top 10 of the Empretec Women in Business awards nominees, the first time a Zambian entrepreneur was on the list.

Back then, Angelica was a member of the Zambia Development Agency which ran courses for entrepreneurs. It invited Angelica to apply for the Empretec training workshop. The outcome was "wonderful, life-changing training," she said.

Here she learned how to infuse greater quality into her product offering to better meet customers' preferences, and in doing so, raised the quality to international standards.

Now she is passing her knowledge onwards by helping young entrepreneurs to develop their businesses, no matter what level they are at.

Angelica describes herself as an entrepreneur and a social activist. She loves to help other people progress, take up opportunities for better income, and ensure natural resources are preserved.

FIND OUT MORE

https://www.facebook.com/angelicamagdallen.rumsey

An artist sowing joy

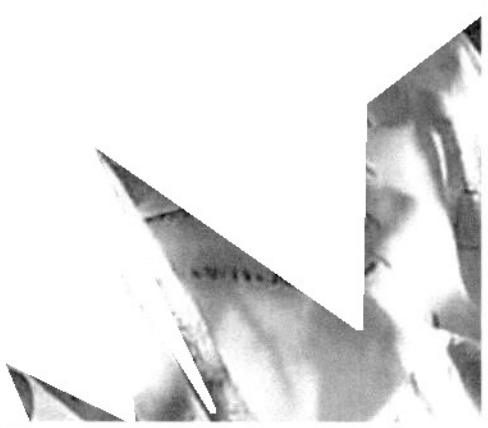

Tracy Antoinette Greene Douglas was always a creator. Her journey took her from the hustle and bustle of New York to running a relaxing creative retreat with her husband in Guyana where she is able to flow her own creativity into the lives of others.

Tracy Antoinette Greene Douglas and her husband Warren were sitting in their back yard in Charlotte, North Carolina talking about soap and wine – their "maker" experiences. That conversation would lead the couple to manufacture wine from North Carolina peaches, and eventually the establishment of the Pandama Retreat and Winery in Guyana.

This is a far cry from Jamaica Queens, New York, where Tracy was born. The couple co-founded the retreat with the goal of pursuing their many artisanal skills, creating a sustainable business, and chasing joy.

The retreat – a center for the creative arts – offers space for people to enjoy and relax, especially during weekends. Pandama produces vinegars, fruit soaps, scrubs and butters, art and art clothing.

Tracy loves to do things that bring joy to her life. She is multitalented. She can cook, paint, make jewellery. She does tie dye, hosts guests at her retreat centre, and runs the business operations. She is also a Reiki Master and Shift Coach.

Her fun-loving attitude and creativity are a big selling point for the business and she believes this is due to her mother who always supported her skills development and artistic expression, but also instilled entrepreneurial competencies in her. These were later reinforced by Empretec training.

AN ARTISTIC APPROACH

A major part of Tracy's work involves surface design, which includes working with fabric. For almost 30 years, Tracy has been a master in the art of tie dye. She utilises dye-friendly fabrics to create colourful masterpieces.

She says that whatever she undertakes, she always tries to give her best. For example, when she creates the tie dye T-shirts, she does it so skilfully that her work is now internationally recognised. "When I cook food, I do it with so much joy and wholeheartedness that it moves people." She combines art with spirituality and according to her, a strong spiritual foundation keeps you moving ahead. Her spirituality, she says, give her universal tools like happiness, creativity, the ability to live in the present, and to hold no attachment to negative thoughts.

TRACY ANTOINETTE GREENE DOUGLAS
Co-owner of Pandama Retreat, Winery & Center for the Creative Arts
GUYANA

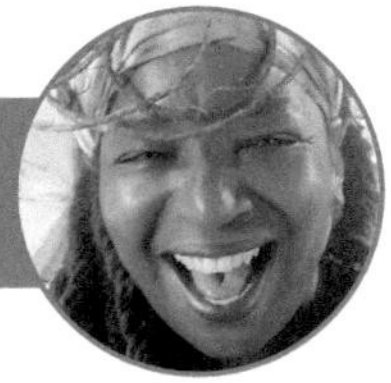

"Everyone needs to express their viewpoints and ideas. There are steadfast and valuable lessons learnt while you make mistakes, but no need to hold on to them," says Tracy.

A simple life lesson, she says, serves as an example. One day Tracy baked a cake with pudding. The pudding sunk into the cake. She had promised her guests a dessert, so she just put the cake and pudding in the oven and baked it anyway. Her guests applauded her for the delicious dessert, that was the outcome.

"We should not be hard on ourselves, we should try to leave out this hardness, we should not give in to other people's opinion, just do what your heart and mind tell you to do. Try to make the best out of the turmoil, and that is creativity," she says.

This approach has served the business well. Tracy says her and Warren have created a strong foundation in their business which is about work and play. "There is a nice rhythm around our daily lifestyles and it's not just business," she explains.

Resources, she believes are abundant. "Never think there is no money. There is nothing wrong in taking loans for expanding your business, but people get so preoccupied with repaying those loans that they lose their creative skills in the process. Make a little bit of money first, then invest and then make money again and re-invest," she advises. This is how she has scaled her business.

RECOGNITION JOY

In 2014, Tracy was nominated for the Empretec Women in Business awards. She was selected for her entrepreneurial spirit and innovative business. The Empretec experience completely changed Tracy's life.

She says the award and network generated "extreme levels of validation that were incredibly fascinating and interesting.

"I interacted with many like-minded women, and we spoke about how to take one's passion and create economic value out of it," she says.

The long-term impacts of the training and award continue to ripple in Tracy's life. She says she is always able to evaluate and see how things are working or not and then move on, a critical business skill.

FIND OUT MORE

http://www.pandamaretreat.com/
https://www.instagram.com/artbyagoddess/
https://www.instagram.com/pandamaretreat/
https://www.facebook.com/artwineandblackwater

Mrs Robot: A digital STEM engine

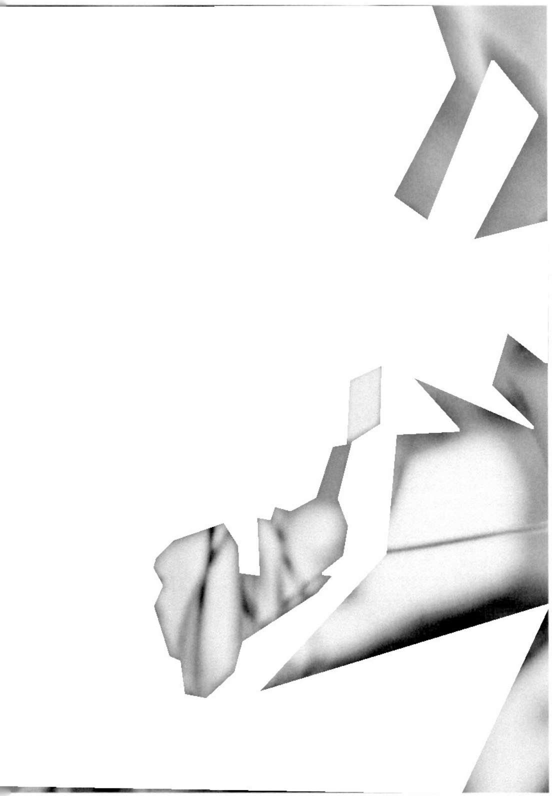

The education sector has not kept pace with technological change. But one Jordanian woman is bent on re-shaping curriculums to ensure that it does; and that young people are future-proofed and ready for the digital age.

In the early part of the past decade, Lama Sha'sha'a saw a massive gap in the education market. Despite the fact that the world had changed, she found that the education children get today is virtually the same as the one she received decades earlier. Something needed to change.

This realisation set Lama on a path that led to her co-founding the International Robotics Academy (IRA) in 2014, a private institution that specialises in robotics and science, technology, engineering and mathematics (STEM) education designed specifically for children.

It is a place where children and youth can test their potential as designers, coders, robot makers and entrepreneurs, while creating smart solutions to bring in a change to the world.

"I saw that children's curiosity and interest in technology could be their motive to learn and create a positive impact," she says.

"The programmes we roll out focus on building capacities and skills needed in the digital age, targeting students between the ages 6-16 years old, and professional development programme for students 19 and above."

"I decided to open up the International Robotics Academy because I wanted to empower children, and make sure they are well equipped for the digital age," Lama says.

Since 2014, the academy has supported schools, educators, parents and students with curriculums and enrichment programmes and opened the stage for children and youth to voice their ideas and pitch their prototypes focused on solving pressing problems. What's more, all prototypes need to address at least one of the United Nations' sustainable development goals.

The academy has edified more than 15,000 students in 10 international schools in Jordan, running more than 900 courses in the past seven years.

Lama is planning on expanding to other countries to identify pools of talents across the globe, focusing on encouraging girls to create technology, robotics, and be part of STEM fields. Her work saw her win a 2018 Empretec Women in Business award.

LAMA SHA'SHA'A
Co-founder of the International Robotics Academy
JORDAN

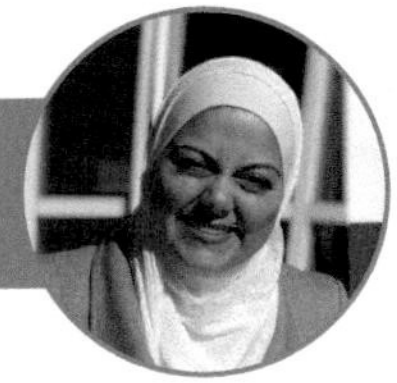

THE PUSH FACTOR

Since leaving school, Lama noticed that the missing key in the education sector was nurturing creativity and holistic development.

Watching her own children learn was a major prompt for her. She started studying her children's syllabus and became focused on what was needed to catch and hold a child's attention. She observed that her children were completely absorbed by technology and saw an opportunity to connect with them in their "language".

Over time Lama created a fully-fledged programme where children could build something with technology by playing the role of a designer, coder, marketer, or entrepreneur. She hired a group of engineers who could help with robotics and created an easy to apply and run curriculum with them that's now taught at the academy.

A TRAINING OPPORTUNITY

Before she launched the academy, in 2012, Lama was part of the Business Development Center (BDC), the local host of the Empretec programme in Jordan, where she attended the Empretec training workshop. Lama says it enlightened her and gave her a better clarity about the project before it was born.

Lama was initially hesitant to start her business, as she lacked technical know-how for the setup. But her coach guided her and reminded her of the skills she had gained at Empretec. Fast-forward to 2022 and Lama is now a member of the BDC board, helping people like her to scale their businesses.

Lama is a proponent of using failure to learn. "Usually, in schools, we learn that you should always get it right. In fact the learning journey is designed around knowing the answers, while in real life we experiment and should not be afraid of trying and failing," she says. "Nobody knows it all. Sometimes I needed to unlearn what I have learnt in the past, re-learn new methods."

RECOGNIZED TALENT

Lama's incredible idea and the impact it had has garnered her considerable international attention. Recently, she was invited to attend the 2022 Fortune-US Department of State Global Women's Mentoring Partnership.

Her Women in Business award came with a special fellowship from the IMD Business School in Lausanne. She said the programme was life-changing. Following this, she was granted another scholarship to continue with a new course on digital excellence.

This, she says, was a turning point as she built relations with people who are successful in their industries, met people from across the globe, and connected with executives in the giants of digital transformation.

Right now Lama wants to scale her TechGirls program globally to focus more on building girls' self-efficacy and self confidence in Robotics and STEM fields for their future careers in the digital age.

FIND OUT MORE

https://www.instagram.com/shashaalama/
https://twitter.com/lama_shashaa
https://www.linkedin.com/in/international-robotics-academy-134ba9b9/

Producing sweets from heaven

Jordanian chocoholic Lina Hundaileh was faced with a fork in the road when she lost her job at a German chocolate factory: sink or swim. The entrepreneur took a leap. She applied her job experience to a new venture to produce chocolate and its by-products in Jordan.

Lina Hundaileh is passionate about chocolate, and who can blame her? But in this case her passion is a pretty productive occupation that started as a prototype and has grown into a multi-brand company.

When the German chocolate factory she was working at closed down in 1992, Lina had to make a plan: look for a job or start her own business. She chose the latter, and decided to open her own chocolate factory.

Sounds simple, right? Not as easy as it seems, she would learn. But endurance and a love for chocolate drove her to drum up support from every quarter.

After writing to every chocolate company she knew without response, she finally caught a break when a company in Cyprus agreed to discuss her business plan. They were impressed with her strategy and forged a collaboration. So Chocolography was born.

CHOCOLATE - HAPPINESS YOU CAN EAT

Lina wanted her chocolate product to be both healthy and ethical. She differentiated herself in the market by creating sugarless chocolates for people with blood sugar disorders and low calorie chocolates for those on diet.

It took her two years to start manufacturing chocolates "Tops" her chocolate brand fortified with vitamins and minerals. Tops enriches sugar free chocolate bars with B12, zinc, calcium and iron after Lina discovered a high percent of Jordanians were deficient in these minerals.

"A bar of 60 grams of chocolate has the daily recommended allowances of the minerals required for an adult," says Lina. Her innovation has been studied by professors and academics interested in healthy chocolate as a commercial opportunity.

Lina has also expanded her offering to include personalised chocolates, creating a demand that never existed before in Jordan. The chocolates are embossed with names and given as gifts for different occasions such as weddings and engagements.

LINA HUNDAILEH
Chocolography
JORDAN

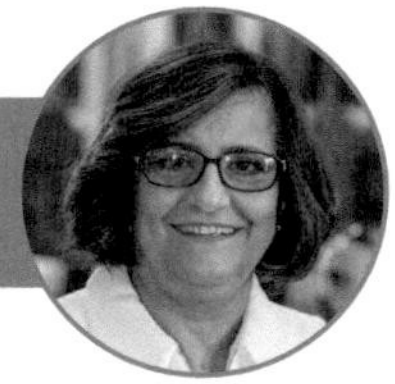

Chocolography is now one of the best chocolate boutiques in Jordan. Lina was nominated in 2010 for an UNCTAD Empretec Women in Business award.

A SWEET CHALLENGE

One of the first challenges Lina had to deal with was perception. No-one in Jordan believed it was possible to produce chocolates in the country. Lina had to convince the locals that the chocolates she produced were high quality.

She invested a lot in driving awareness. Gradually, her chocolates found place on the shelves of local supermarkets. But few knew the chocolates actually originated in Jordan.

Lina also started her business in a crowded market with many competitors. "I wondered how I could compete with such big giants," Lina says. "I just had pennies for marketing and exports. A business person looks at their business from a monetary point of view, but a true entrepreneur puts their heart and passion into any business, before thinking about the monetary gain."

Lina did this and the gains are evident today mainly because she was able to create a niche for her brand. Lina says, "It wasn't because I was strong, but because I had done my homework, had a vision and a convincing story to tell, it was because I found my why."

"Women should concentrate on their goal. We should define our whys - find our passion, pursue it and having gratitude helps a lot."

BECOMING AN EMPRETECA

Lina says that her coach from Brazil recommended that she join Empretec as a trainer to share her experiences and skills. Lina agreed and started training others, but also bringing new ideas to the course.

Many trainers start as trainees and Lina says the Empretec training made her more disciplined and encouraged her to produce new products and variants. Prior to Empretec, she says she had the habit of procrastinating.

The Empretec training, she says, made her more diligent and helped her to increase her productivity and sales. "The Empretec programme taught me not to procrastinate and to set goals with deadline and work with dedication to achieve those goals," says Lina.

Today Lina gives back. She has connected with many women entrepreneurs with whom she shares her stories, listens to their stories, helps them to dig within themselves to realise their strengths, and change their mindsets. She says her passion has now shifted to mentoring.

FIND OUT MORE

https://www.instagram.com/chocolographyjo/
https://www.linkedin.com/in/lina-hundaileh-062468/
https://www.facebook.com/ChocolographyJo/

A wizard at waste management

María Carlota Guevara loves nature more than most. Her vision for the circular economy has led to a small revolution in El Salvadorian waste management. Women have been empowered, waste has been recycled and micro-economies have been created because of TOKA.

TOKA CasaVerde in El Salvador promotes sustainable green spaces. Its genesis story lies at the heart of nature, but its goal is to tackle and better manage waste. It was started by pioneering entrepreneur María Carlota Guevara who wanted to protect nature while empowering women.

María set up TOKA to specialise in recycling inorganic and other non-biodegradable waste, which is collected, sorted, recycled, repurposed and commercialised.

TOKA means to sow or to plant, in María's native nahuatl language. This is exactly what the company is doing: sowing seeds of change and doing so with intent to help women and nature along the way.

"Nature," says María, "is the gift we have all been given." She is intent on ensuring that gift is shared among everyone. "Consumerism must be sustainable and this can be done by following the traditional processes that are respectful of the environment," said the 62-year-old social entrepreneur.

THE WASTE PROBLEM

At an early age, María was conscious of the growing waste problem around her. She was constantly thinking of ways to recycle and upcycle the waste. It was evident to her that the logical way to proceed was to use waste materials for other processes, which in turn would reduce the negative impact on the environment and generate an income for producers.

TOKA's workforce – of which 85% are women – recycles wood and textile waste into refurbished products, and the employees add plants to these products to build mini-gardens and "living walls". TOKA has an online store where they sell their handicrafts.

Even though sourcing funding is difficult, mainly because people don't understand what María is doing with her social enterprise, she says they have managed to become an income generating enterprise. Now TOKA is certified by the El Salvador Ministry of Environment to provide training and environmental awareness seminars.

MARÍA CARLOTA GUEVARA
Owner of TOKA Casaverde
EL SALVADOR

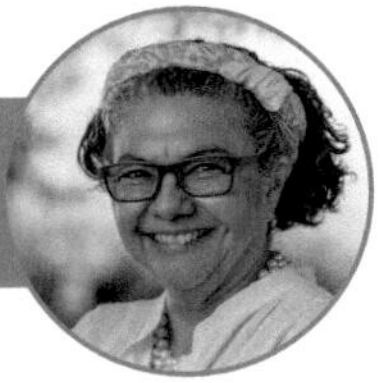

A COMPETENCY BASE

In 2012, María was among the top 10 finalists for the Empretec Women in Business awards for her innovative project. She says her "business life can be divided into before and after Empretec."

The training, she says, was not only about business techniques, but more about the human qualities that could be put into practice in the entrepreneurial process.

After the training, she was able to improve the quality of her work using the techniques she had learned. "The knowledge helped me to create greater leverage for my business," María said.

As part of her Women in Business award, she was invited to visit a waste processing plant in Edmonton, Canada. She was amazed to see their zero-waste processes.

"It was astonishing to realise how all kinds of waste were being efficiently treated in the plant, everything was clean and there were no foul smells," María says.

She also travelled to Brazil, where she met with a woman entrepreneur who recycles organic cotton, using natural dyes and sustainable packages for her products. María was amazed and has flowed some of the inspiration she gained from these moments into TOKA's creations.

She constantly applies the core competencies she learned during the Empretec training, but the two most applicable lessons are to live a meaningful life and never give up, she says. "I learned that there is nothing that can really stop me, challenges can be transformed into opportunities and we should not give up," she says.

A prime example is the COVID-19 crisis, which was actually good for her business. Before the pandemic, people were still becoming accustomed to online shopping but the pandemic ended up boosting her online sales tremendously. She admits that nowadays everyone prefers to buy online.

María is still dreaming big even in her later years as an entrepreneur and she has shifted focus to food insecurity and harnessing nature's solutions.

"The processes in the natural chains are perfect but when one shackle is broken, problems arise. So we must take care of it, to avoid insecurity," she says.

She also thinks women are part of the solution for saving nature. "Women are just incredible, nothing can stop them from achieving if they set their heart and mind on something. Women are better equipped and skilled with greater managerial traits for starting a business of their own – we should do it. Do not give up. The power is within you."

FIND OUT MORE

https://www.instagram.com/tokacasaverde/
https://www.facebook.com/tokacasaverde

Selling food as medicine

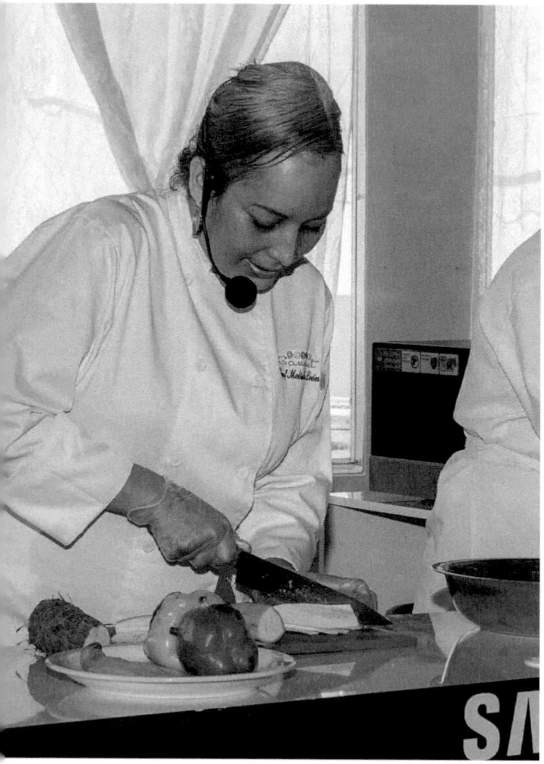

It's hard to imagine today, but once upon a time gluten-free products were hard to come by, while millions struggled with the allergy to gluten. Chef Melissa de León recognized this challenge more than a decade ago. She's been helping people ever since.

Melissa de León is a chef on a culinary course to create healthy food that sustains – and even fixes – people. Melissa started her food venture in 2010, selling gluten-free products. She believes food is not just for energy and enjoyment, "it's a medicine too".

Since 2010, when she started Panama Gourmet, she's been an active advocate for local, organic and healthy food cooked with soul. Her gluten-free company did well until 2018 when she shifted focus, parting ways with her business partners to start a new business, Sol Kitchen.

Sol means sun in Spanish and Melissa sees the sun as the primary creator of all nourishment through light and energy. Sol Kitchen is a "central kitchen" or a professional kitchen where good cooking and eating habits are taught to food producers and other people. Melissa wants to teach people how to eat well, especially in the rural areas and countryside of Panama.

The goal is to treasure and protect traditional culinary heritage, which is under threat of being lost. Melissa's company helps protect the heritage not only by providing a learning space, but also purchasing local products directly from traders and teaching people how to grow the key ingredients for food production.

She says the idea of working together in a central place reduces costs and encourages and builds community. "Never be afraid to do what you have decided. It doesn't matter even if you fail, try till you achieve your goal, never give up," she says.

This motto and approach has served her well over her career as a chef. Outside of her businesses she has also headlined a popular television cooking show broadcast across Latin America, featuring women chefs from across the region, focusing on traditional and innovative desserts. She also regularly shared her cooking adventures on the cookingdiva.net blog.

She has something else brewing in the kitchen too. She and some partners are growing dragon fruit, a delicious and nutritious fruit originally grown in China and Costa Rica, which they aim to popularise on menus.

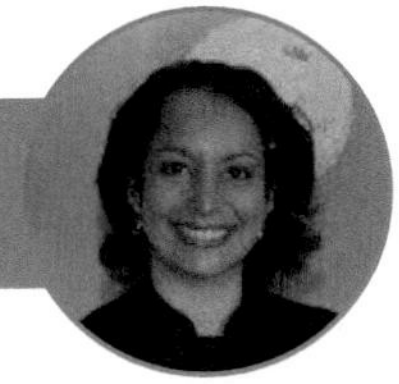

MELISSA DE LEÓN
Owner of Panama Gourmet now Sol Kitchen
PANAMA

EMPRETEC'S IMPACT

Melissa De León won the 2012 Empretec Women in Business award for her work. She said Empretec helped her orientate and succeed.

"I learned how to build a business, utilise ideas, and correct all the problems in my business," she says.

"The most important aspect is that this training changes your mindset, as you learn lifelong concepts and competencies for any current or future businesses you may want to build."

Melissa said Empretec taught her things she didn't know about before such as investigating the market, developing different strategies, how to improve people's lives and livelihood prospects; and most importantly how to create a profitable business.

She also learned how to do systematic planning and monitoring of her business, set milestones and learn the techniques to achieve them.

She gained knowledge of how to plan strategically to achieve her goals. Since then, she has learnt to organise herself to succeed.

Empretec taught her every aspect of business needed to drive success, she says.

That accomplishment means that Melissa has been recognised regularly by her government and community.

She was featured at the launch of the Panama Ministry of Micro, Small and Medium-sized Enterprises' new entrepreneurship centre. She is also a part of the mentor group in the City of Knowledge in Panama, mentoring young women entrepreneurs sharing her experience and knowledge.

FIND OUT MORE

https://twitter.com/cookingdiva
https://www.linkedin.com/in/melissa-de-leon-bb14483/
https://www.facebook.com/chefmelissadeleon/

Women Redefining Agricultural Businesses

The 2022 food crisis put into sharp focus the importance of food security. Global food security – already under pressure after two years of disruption due to the COVID-19 pandemic, extenuating climate factors and rolling worldwide droughts – has been exacerbated by the war in Ukraine. Ironically, hunger, which was falling before 2015, has risen over the past 7 years. In 2005 the number of undernourished people was 811 million. In 2020 the number was back at 811 million people, despite gains in the interleading years which saw the number of hungry people fall as low as 607 million, says the Food and Agricultural Organization. In 2022, the FAO predicts, because of the high costs of food staples, about 1.6 billion people cannot ensure there will be enough food on their tables to eat.

We need more entrepreneurs and farmers, especially in the breadbaskets of the world, working to find solutions to the issue of local and global food security. There is huge opportunity in the field of food technology, agri-tech and integration of small farmers into the global supply chain which can ensure a more sustainable and inclusive production. Many women work as subsistence farmers but are excluded from formal structures because of their gender and bias against women farmers. But in some nations, women entrepreneurs and business-owners are seeing the opening, and moving to come up with sustainable solutions to improve food security and alleviate poverty. In this section we meet two women who are working to make a difference in agriculture and using innovative means to do so.

Firstly, we hear from a biochemist from India fascinated by bees, who wants to produce pure, unadulterated honey to harness its medical and health benefits. Then we explore the story of a Tanzanian fresh produce exporter and agri-tech entrepreneur who is helping match farmers with local and global markets while training them to help improve production.

A biochemist's pursuit to help us live right

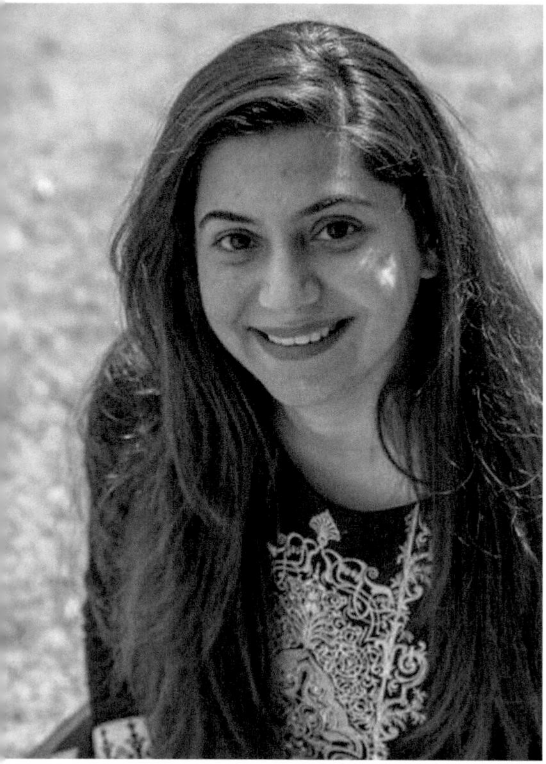

Kayan Motashaw is a biochemist and entrepreneur. Founder of LivRite Foods, she's also a busy bee. Her honey brand, Beelicious, is a premium health brand free from all the bad things that occasionally make its way into this popular product.

Honey is not always as pure as we think it is. In fact, it is one of the most faked foods in the world. Honey's often diluted with liquids such as beet syrup or corn syrup. In India, where Kayan Motashaw lives, a 2021 report by the Indian research organization the Centre for Science and Environment (CSE), found that 77% of local honey samples were adultered with sugar syrup.

This learning drove Kayan to change the honey production industry in India. Kayan is the founder of LivRite a new and emerging Indian company in the beekeeping space.

Her brand, Beelicious, sells premium, pure, responsibly-sourced, traceable and authentic honey – guaranteed! She wants to ensure consumers are buying real honey that retains all the nutritional and medicinal qualities.

Kayan's interest in bees and honey emerged while she was studying to be a biochemist. She wanted to explore the beneficial biochemical properties of honey such as moisture, ash, acidity, specific sugars, and potassium. She was also intrigued by the cultural and medicinal properties of ancient and non-commercial honey.

"People influenced by western culture have lost track of how honey could heal a person from head to toe without them consuming chemicals, anti-biotics, or any medicine that could have adverse effects on the immune system," says Kayan.

A JOURNEY TO THE SWEET CENTRE

Her curiosity around honey and bees led her to travel to many places, meet different beekeepers, and gather valuable information. Her research was congruent with the CSE's findings. Most honey in India is manufactured, processed, overheated, and often adulterated.

She discovered there was only one existing variant of honey in India. Nobody offered the unifloral variants like leechi, eucalyptus, and kashmiri acacia. She travelled to many states of North India and met many beekeepers to collect more information about their extraction process and to build a network of producers.

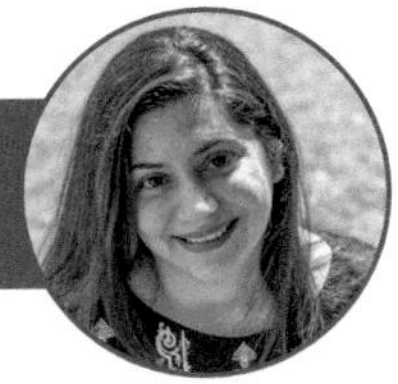

KAYAN MOTASHAW
Founder of LivRite
INDIA

They were reluctant to share all the details initially, she says, and were not ready to accept the new techniques suggested. These beekeepers were extracting honey in a hurry without allowing natural sealing with proper natural beeswax, which resulted in an unpalatable and raw flavour.

The challenges were significant. There were also no proper mechanisms to test the quality of honey on the field. Most of the farmers expected immediate cash payment on a purchase. Many of them did not have a bank account, which made it difficult to transact, Kayan said. This was a challenge as she needed to confirm the quality before making payment for the honey.

She decided to import special test kits from the United States, which helped to check the basic parameters in the quality of honey. Only after these quality tests were approved, honey was collected and sent to her facility.

Surpassing all hurdles, especially gaining the trust of beekeepers in the field, paved the way to the establishment of LivRite. The result is her brand Beelicious, a pure and distinctive honey which delivers the health benefits expected of honey. The golden, delicious liquid also empowered beekeepers around India.

"Farming is seasonal, and after the harvest, many farmers struggle. Beekeeping is a year-round activity where they can seasonally migrate the boxes and generate income throughout the year. That felt very fulfilling," says Kayan. Her company now helps farmers and beekeepers earn revenue all year around.

A GROWTH OUTLOOK

Kayan is expanding – slowly but surely, she says. This growth came in the form of a bold move to start exporting to the Middle East, induced in part by the risk-taking aptitude nurtured through Empretec training.

Before Empretec, she says she was wary of taking decisions. But after the workshop, she decided that she had to take complete responsibility for every outcome. Also, she started taking decisions irrespective of her fear of the outcome. "Empretec has had a remarkable effect on the growth of my business," Kayan says.

Now she plans to diversify into the wellness sector, to tap honey's many benefits including supporting gut (digestive) health, regulating blood sugar, and improving immunity. Kayan wants to manufacture health tonics and foods that feature honey as the main ingredient.

Kayan believes in taking big leaps and attributes this quality to her father who taught her to take risks. "At some point, just believe in yourself and move forward in life," says Kayan.

FIND OUT MORE

https://www.beelicious.in/
https://www.linkedin.com/in/kayanmotashaw/
https://www.facebook.com/kayan.motashaw

Tanzania's agricultural inspiration

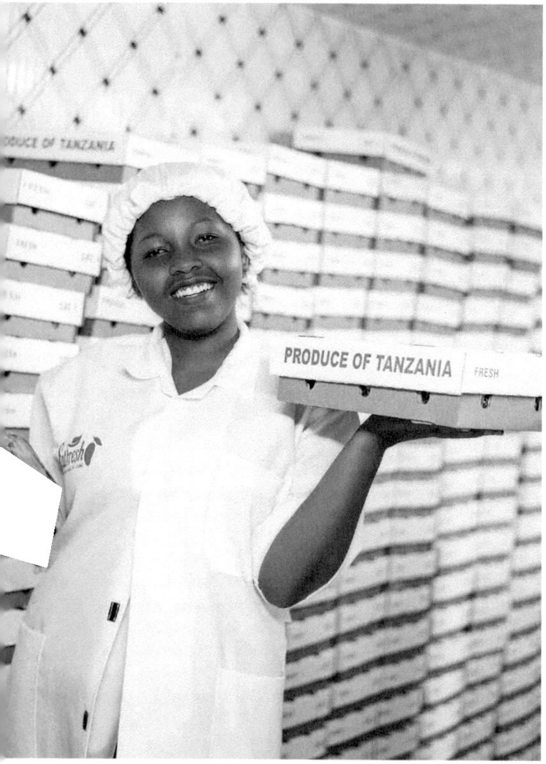

Hadija Jabiri is a matchmaker at heart. Her work's taken her deep into the world of fresh produce production and export. She's even delved into the world of agri-tech, starting an app to help connect farmers with agricultural specialists.

Farming found Hadija Jabiri, not the other way around. She had never considered a career as a farmer, but after watching a television programme about farming during her first year of university, she was inspired to get her hands into the earth to help meet the food security demands of a growing population.

The result is a woman-founded and run agricultural company that helps women and small farmers sell their produce. In fact, Hadija is the chief executive of two farmer-focused Tanzanian businesses: GBRI Business Solutions Ltd (also known as Eat Fresh Tanzania) and Agriedo Ltd., a company that produces agri-tech solutions.

Eat Fresh Tanzania is a huge exporter of the country's fresh produce. They grow and export vegetables to Europe. But farming, says Hadija, is not easy. Most women in Tanzania are subsistence farmers and make up the bulk of farmers in the country. Yet they are excluded in several ways including from finding access to land, finances, markets and new techniques.

"In Tanzania, rural farmers face numerous challenges; most of them are at the lower end of the pyramid. There are few women farmers who are at the top level," she says. "Among the reasons are that banks shy away from lending to agricultural projects, as it is considered a risky business."

When GBRI started, they grew traditional vegetables such as onions and cucumbers and distributed them to local markets. They started to expand and before long were exporting non-traditional vegetables like sugar snap, snow peas, French beans, and baby corn to European countries. But the COVID-19 pandemic put a handbrake on this expansion.

A PANDEMIC PIVOT

Hadija had big plans for 2020. GBRI had secured a new investor and a significant project with funding from the Dutch government to increase their resources from 500 to 2,000 farmers.

Then the COVID-19 pandemic arrived and put a dampener on their plans. As borders closed and the workforce was asked to stay home, Hadija had to think of a way to keep going.

HADIJA JABIRI
Founder, CEO Eat Fresh Tanzania & Agriedo Ltd.
TANZANIA

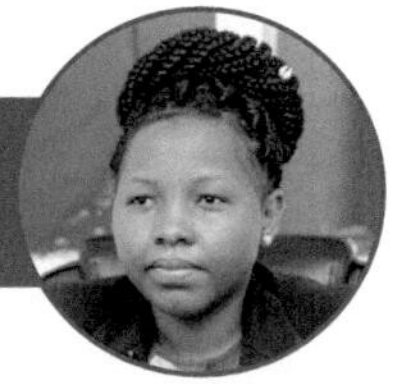

An idea struck. Instead of exporting, it was time to serve the domestic market again, Hadija thought. She changed the company's marketing strategy from export-led to a focus on local sales.

She decided to get into fruit selling. GBRI bought fruits from local suppliers and ripened them in their warehouse. They used their existing resources to sell and deliver fruits domestically.

Hadija also decided to pivot in a new direction. She created a new company called Agriedo Ltd., an agri-tech company focused on developing technologies for small-size farmers.

Their online application, Bwaanashamba (Swahili for agronomist), helps farmers access the services of nearby agronomists. It's transformed farmers' productivity, says Hadija.

Hadija credits Empretec training for her appetite for taking calculated risks. "As an entrepreneur you need to be resilient and not give up and think how we can adapt and be flexible," says Hadija, Tanzania's youngest horticulturalist.

MISTAKES ARE PART OF THE JOURNEY

When Hadija started her business, she recalled making many mistakes. She had no agricultural background, lacked knowledge of business processes and technical know-how.

While several trials and errors – including losing money – were hard fees to pay, she eventually learned that mistakes are steppingstones to success, she says.

Her accounting background along with earlier business failures helped her to build a foundation when venturing into horticulture.

Now GBRI is Global GAP (Good Agricultural Practice) certified and has a labour force made up of 80% women. GBRI has trained more than 500 small-size farmers, not only giving them the market for their produce, but also connecting them to a wider network that is interested in supporting women.

Agriedo is also running an incubation hub, which showcases technological ideas to women. The hub incubates emerging ideas to the point they become viable businesses.

Her commitment to supporting women and farmers has led to several accolades and recognition. In 2020, Hadija was one of the top ten finalists in UNCTAD's Empretec Women in Business award.

She is also the recipient of the 2021 Feed the Future Growing Women's Entrepreneurship (GroWE) award. Her advice to aspiring entrepreneurs is be prepared.

"Go out and explore various options for support. Ask for support from the right people. Understand what the customer needs and give them exactly what they need instead of what you want. Stick to your lane and believe in yourself despite the obstacles you face."

FIND OUT MORE

https://www.instagram.com/hadija_jabiri/
https://twitter.com/hadija_jabiry1
https://www.linkedin.com/in/hadija-jabiri-857754b2/
https://www.facebook.com/hadija.jabiry

Developing the Skills of Future Generations

Many entrepreneurs see the long-term potential of sharing what they know with future entrepreneurs and young people. It's extremely important to think of legacy and impact when building a sustainable and inclusive business. Enterprise owners who do so often reap the fruits of their reward and see impacts ripple through their communities.

Training and skills development are a crucial part of uplifting not only employees but entire ecosystems and economies. The development of skills enhances employability and labor productivity and helps countries to become more competitive.

The World Bank argues that investment in a high-quality workforce can create a virtuous cycle, where relevant and quality skills enable productivity growth and foreign direct investment, which result in more and better jobs for the current workforce and more public and private investment in the education and training system. But many countries struggle to deliver on the promise of skills development.

There are huge gaps in basic literacy and numeracy of working-age populations. The World Bank says that 750 million people aged 15+ (or 18% of the global population) report being unable to read and write.

In this section we focus on women who have taken a long view of their potential impact and invested heavily in training, often pivoting initial entrepreneurial ventures into skills development initiatives. They are operating in the dimension of legacy.

We hear from the owner of a major Malaysian academy who worked her way up through a company and then flipped into training. We learn from a South African businesswoman turned mentor who's helping entrepreneurs manage their mindset. From The Gambia comes a tale of a banker who left the industry to start a hairdressing academy that scaled into a bigger skills development engine. Finally, we explore the story of a Ugandan woman who built a school to ensure the girl-child and young people have the chance of education.

From chambermaid to C-suite executive

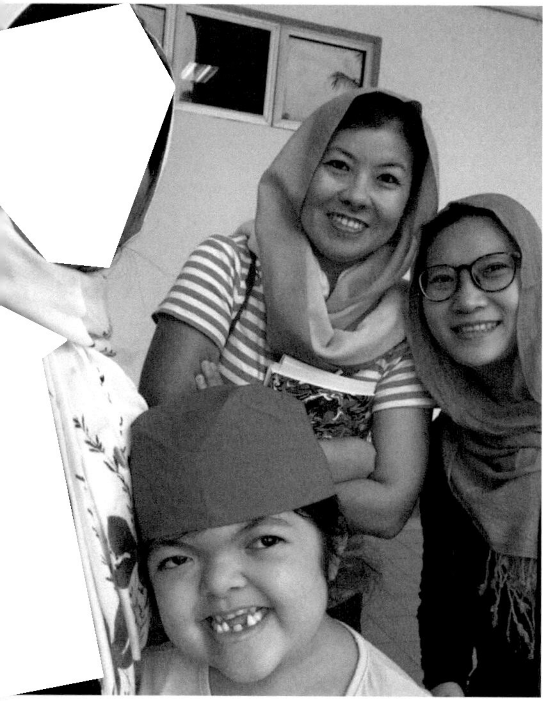

Sandra Anne Ghouse's incredible ascent from the bottom to the top shows how determination, commitment, and sound mentorship can change everything. She rose to the top position of the company she was in and is now a serial entrepreneur and trainer-mentor herself.

Sandra Anne Ghouse didn't think much of herself, or her skills set, when she was young. She considered herself rather average and unremarkable compared with her Malaysian peers. But there is nothing unremarkable about Sandra.

She is a powerhouse that worked her way up through the ranks to become head of the business she joined as a tele-salesperson years back.

Before that, she worked as a chambermaid in a hotel to make ends meet and to pay for her school. Cleaning hotel rooms made her a salary of less than $50 per month. She used to take two buses to travel one hour to work daily and worked 11 hours a day.

However, it was her part time job as a telephone operator that changed her trajectory. The owner of the business took her under his wing. He had a similar story of ascent himself. "I owe most of my success today to him," she says.

"He taught me to see life from a different perspective", Sandra reflects. It was his strict training that laid the strong foundation of who she is today. One day, he unexpectedly pushed her to train other secretaries on time management.

The one-on-one classes grew from four people to seven and then to 25 people, and finally to training many people throughout the country. "I found my voice and discovered that I was able to make presentations, and develop training and development programs," Sandra says.

Sandra climbed the ranks within the company, where she worked for 26 years. She eventually became a senior leader and then was promoted to the C-suite as a director.

AN ENTREPRENEURIAL LEAP

Sandra decided to start experimenting with different ventures later in life. Together with a client she started a wellness center for women called Fleur De Vie, or Flower of Life. The business didn't succeed but Sandra was hooked on creating her own enterprise. So, she focused on her skills

SANDRA ANNE GHOUSE
Owner of 3E Training & Education Sdn Bhd
MALAYSIA

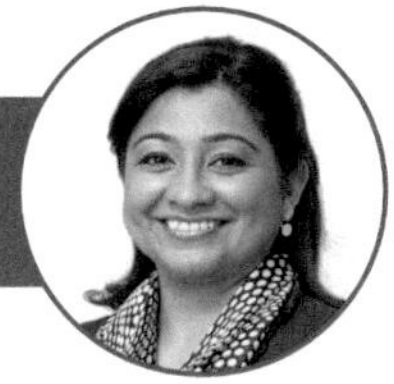

and experience, and opened 3E Training & Education, her training business, in a heavily saturated and competitive Malaysian marketplace. Ironically, it was COVID-19 that gave her an edge.

During the pandemic, she reached out to government agencies, and announced that they can conduct online training.

This gave her company a constant flow of business and connections in the digital space who wanted to train online. Sandra targeted vulnerable groups and refugees, most of whom had little education or experience. Within a few months they were taught how to become successful micro-entrepreneurs, by being curious and seeking opportunities.

A PENNY DROPS

Even though she was a business-woman for more than 26 years, Sandra says it was through the Empretec programme that she got a structured and in depth understanding of the 10 critical entrepreneurial competencies needed to build a sustainable and successful business.

She says Empretec showed her strengths and weaknesses clearly; and how to acquire and implement competencies. She believes that "if we don't build a sustainable and profitable business that runs on its own without the owner being present daily, then we're merely living out our hobby and we're not really entrepreneurs."

Her remarkable journey saw her being recognised in the 2020 Empretec Women in Business awards.

This notch is added to an already full belt of recognition, including her role as Vice President of Membership of the National Association of Women Entrepreneurs in Malaysia.

Even though she is in her 50s, Sandra believes life has just begun. "Age doesn't matter", she says. She has no plans to retire and envisages projects she wants to work on for the next 50 years.

Her dream is to start a "University of Life", where she would like to teach the children her formulae, so they can build a better life for themselves.

Sandra advises women to prioritize their "now". According to her, many women feel that they need to be a submissive, nice person or else they will not be accepted or taken seriously.

This is why Sandra believes in training women to become confident and courageous; and to take responsibility and boost their self-worth.

FIND OUT MORE

https://www.instagram.com/3e_training_education/
https://www.youtube.com/channel/UC_LavWXNHhSlewYIgS9tEJg
https://www.linkedin.com/in/3e-training-and-education-6b4567193/
https://www.facebook.com/3etrain

Turning hindsight into foresight

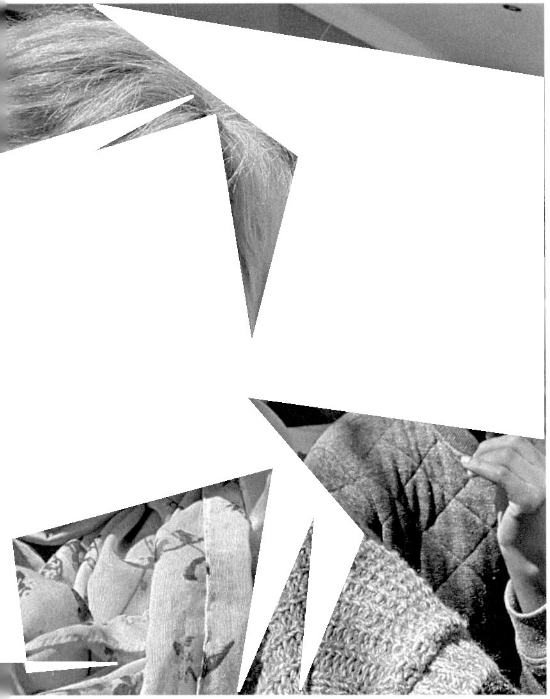

Renay van der Berg had 34 years' experience running her own business under her belt when, after Empretec training, she decided it was time to share those skills and lessons with young South Africans. So she flipped her business into a mentorship initiative and hasn't looked back since 2014.

After more than 30 years running her own enterprise development company, PRoComm, Renay van der Berg made the conscious decision in 2014 to shift her focus to sharing her knowledge. The goal? Inspiring and empowering young, upcoming entrepreneurs using an holistic business approach that concentrates on personal development and mentorship.

Renay was a well-respected businesswoman and strategist in Welkom, South Africa, when at age 50, she decided to make a career turn to concentrate on training. She was responding to the dire need to support entrepreneurs in South Africa.

Though sceptical of her mentoring skills, she realised that many first-time entrepreneurs needed immediate assistance when they planned to open a business. She moved to fill the gap and changed PRoComm's focus.

"About 55% of youth in South Africa are unemployed or have never worked in their first 35 years of their life. One income here sustains an extended family of 11 people," says Renay. She wanted to change that reality by supporting entrepreneurs at the outset of their journey. This, she believes, will help address unemployment and encourage skills development.

"A person with an income has a purpose. They can take care of their family with dignity," she says, adding that a single salary becomes part of an economic chain that supports entire communities.

Armed with this knowledge, Renay's self-appointed mandate is to ensure enterprises are sustainable and stimulate the local economy.

EVEN ENTREPRENEURS NEED BUSINESS TRAINING

Renay benefited from training herself, which she pays forward in her own business. Renay was always connected to South Africa's Small Business Development Agency (SEDA), the national host of Empretec. PRoComm is one of their longest standing service providers and they recommended Renay for the Empretec training.

Empretec's personal entrepreneurial competencies helped her understand and empower other entrepreneurs and approach her business differently.

RENAY VAN DER BERG
PRoComm
SOUTH AFRICA

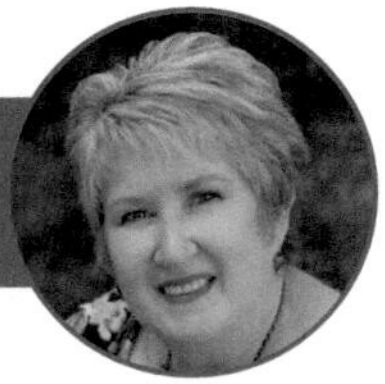

"The two stand-out competencies were networking and self-confidence," she says, and she honed in on these as her main areas for personal and professional growth. She also later flowed learnings about the competencies into her business and onto her clients.

In 2014, she was one of 10 finalists in the Empretec Women in Business awards. It gave her a needed confidence boost. She thought that if she ranked amongst the top 10 in the world, then surely, she possessed enough experience to help others to take their business to the next level – and this inspired the business pivot to focusing on mentorship.

Today, more than 1,000 business owners have benefitted from her interventions. Through mentorship she has changed behaviours, perceptions, and habits to fast-track purposeful impact. This is done by empowering entrepreneurs to become more effective, efficient, productive, and eventually more profitable and sustainable.

A CLOSE AND ABIDING RELATIONSHIP

PRoComm is an extension of Renay's life. She says she is surrounded by youth and she enjoys looking at things from the youth's perspective.

Most of her clients become part of the PRoComm family. "To get a 'thank you' call late at night because the funder delivered machinery, or a message with a success story, is the best reward ever," says Renay. "Mentoring is truly fulfilling."

Renay says her mentorship approach is customisable and flexible. For instance one mentee might need assistance in marketing whereas another needs support on the operations front.

Renay's approach towards them is very flexible and informal, allowing the mentee to steer the process. She helps the entrepreneur create the right mindset and energy to seize opportunities as they come.

She says many young people in South Africa do not have role models to look up to, or guide and inspire them. Lack of inspiration leads to "aspirations", she says. "They aspire to be who they are not, or to do something that is not realistic."

She sometimes plays the role of an older sister. She guides, directs or lends a shoulder when needed. Women are particularly important to Renay. She enjoys when they realise that with the right attitude and mind-set, they can make their dreams come true.

"Start with what you have, where you are. Wait for nobody and nothing. As an entrepreneur, you have to make things happen for yourself," she advises.

FIND OUT MORE

https://procomm.co.za/
https://www.instagram.com/renayvdberg/
https://www.facebook.com/pro.comm.14

Bold banker turned skills maestro

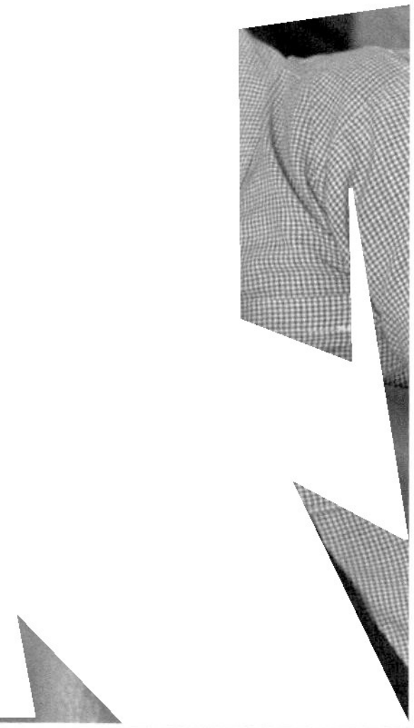

The Gambia's Fatou Gaye left her comfortable banking job to pack a skills punch that is changing the lives of women in the African nation. Now her hairdressing school has flipped to a fully-fledged skills academy that's trained more than 3,000 women, giving them stellar new opportunities.

Fatou Gaye says that while The Gambia is small, "we are big in the way we do things". No-one could embody this truth more than Fatou herself after scaling a small hairdressing school into a major skills development academy that's helping women earn an income and succeed.

The Gaye Njorro Skills Academy is singular in its focus. It aims to keep young people off the streets and contribute to national development. This vision has seen Fatou emerge as a force in social entrepreneurship in The Gambia. In 2016, she won a special award for her work in the Empretec Women in Business awards. It speaks to almost 15 years' worth of work to realise the dream.

A HAIRBRAINED IDEA?

Fatou was always well-educated and she ended up studying finance and banking in the United Kingdom. But while doing so, she needed to generate additional funds and for this she turned to another skill: hairdressing. She started styling hair in her free time.

Later, when she returned home to The Gambia and started a family, this skill was ironically the one that enabled her to be both a mother and earn an income.

She found that banking was too gruelling, and the long hours kept her away from her family. She wanted independence and flexibility. So, she quit her job. With her savings she started her first salon.

Things started slow and took some convincing. Fatou targeted vulnerable young women to work with her. She found her first employee and three others quickly joined her in the salon.

"If a woman is supported, a nation is built because a woman will support another and whoever they come across," she says. She knew that if she wanted to help more girls on the streets, she would need to think big.

She approached the government to find out about the process to open a school. She secured government accreditation and started the Gaye Njorro Skills Academy.

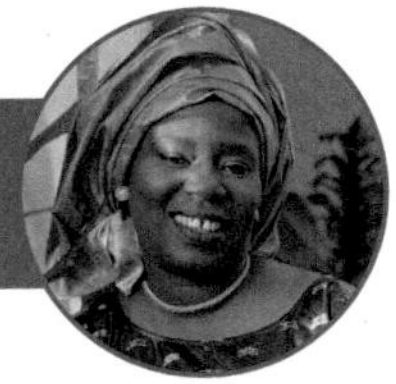

FATOU SAINE GAYE
CEO of the Gaye Njorro Skills Academy
THE GAMBIA

Starting with a skill she was good at – hairdressing – Fatou expanded her centre into a skills academy, teaching several skills to the youth in The Gambia. With help from several NGOs, her academy diversified its training to offer everything from hotel management to tailoring.

As with any beginning, the first half was tough, says Fatou. People in general were reluctant to join and families wanted young women to rather stay at home. She went door-to-door and visited her students' homes to convince their parents and husbands of the benefits of the school.

For example, one time a woman student, who was about to get married, was not allowed to sit for an exam. Fatou convinced her father to grant her permission and had to do the same with the groom-to-be. Fatou spoke to the groom about how his future wife would be able to help him and together they would be empowered and have a better lifestyle with education.

Later, the student's father became an advocate for the school, promoting it in his village. "I wasn't stubborn, but I had a vision," says Fatou. "With persistence and commitment everything is possible."

The academy has been operational for 14 years. It has trained more than 3,000 women and now also includes men in its programmes.

TAKING THE EMPRETEC OPPORTUNITY

Fatou's journey with Empretec has been a long and all-encompassing one, and she has moved from trainee to trainer over the years. Thanks to Empretec she was able to build her business on a solid ground, she says.

The Empretec programme has been the source of a constant push for Fatou. She is an active part of the national initiative and is an Empretec qualified international trainer and youth mentor. She also helped install the Empretec programme in Cameroon and trains different communities in Nigeria.

Winning the Women in Business award opened new opportunities for her. She was coached by an Italian mentor who helped her develop and plan business strategies. "I am not going to just let it go with this Empretec programme, I will be a champion in it," she says.

Today, Fatou trains 300 women every year across the country. The European Union also noticed her work and partnered with her to deliver her youth empowerment projects.

"We are not a poor country. We are a small country rich in human resources, which is very powerful. I believe we can do a lot more if we come and stand together and support each other."

FIND OUT MORE

https://gayenjorroskillsacademy.com/
https://www.facebook.com/fsgaye
https://www.facebook.com/GayeNjorroSkillsAcademy

Education advocate builds edifices

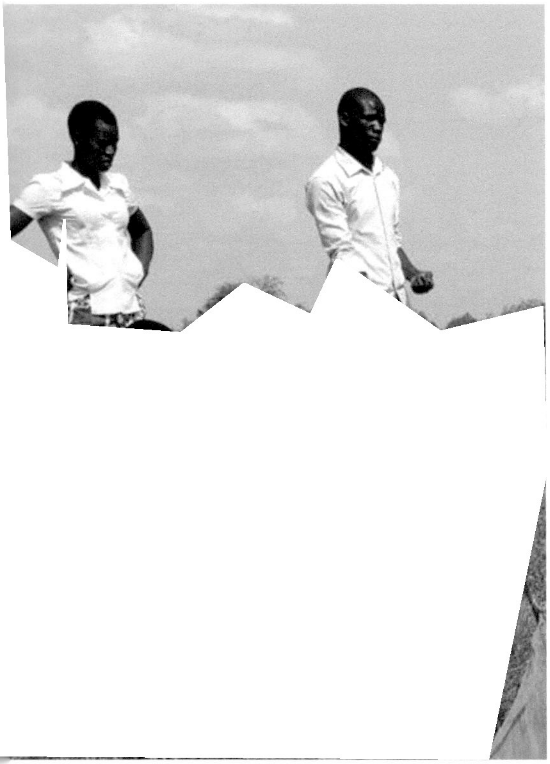

No job was ever too small, menial or hard for Beatrice, who once settled on her vision to build and run a school, was unstoppable in realising it. She used entrepreneurial pursuits to supplement her work toward building the Lira Integrated School.

Education is something that is out of reach for many Ugandan girls. No-one knows this better than Beatrice Ayuru. Her journey to bring access to education has been long and complex, and while it may not have ended in the way she wanted, her impact and legacy continue today.

When she first started thinking about education, she knew a revolution was needed, and she saw building a school as the route to achieving this. But to do so, she needed to start with educating herself. She was the first girl from her village to gain admission to Makerere University – one of her many firsts.

HOW TO SELF-FUND A DREAM

She also knew she needed to make money if she was going to build a school. So she decided to start her first business: growing and selling cassava roots.

While people wondered what an educated woman was doing working in the fields and selling vegetables to the locals, she was using the profits she made to re-invest in a micro-wheelbarrow business. She rented these out at the local bus stations to help carry passengers' luggage. Then she started to work on building the school. Her supportive father loaned her some land, but she still needed capital.

Following her father's advice to understand the education system, Beatrice started by teaching at a school. She learned that there was yet another business opportunity at a neighbouring school. She used her savings from the wheelbarrow business to open a canteen there.

But the going was tough. By 2000 Beatrice was already the mother of four children. She would start her day at 4am working in the canteen, teach at the school and then run the canteen until midnight. All these ventures ultimately helped her fund her school.

AN EDIFICE FOR EDUCATION

While there was some funding available from her savings, it wasn't enough. So Beatrice did everything herself: making bricks, a skill learnt from her

BEATRICE AYURU
Lira Integrated School
UGANDA

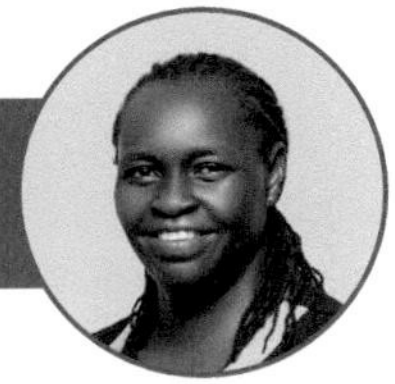

brickmaker father, and building the first walls. In the absence of desks and teaching staff, she started advertising the Lira Integrated School and recruiting teachers.

Who applied? The very teachers she served at the neighbouring school canteen!

The big drawcard was the school's English tuition. Lira was the only school that had English as a subject, taught by Beatrice. Parents started entrusting their children with her.

In the first week, she received 42 applications. By the second week, the number increased to 100 applications.

By the year-end the school was full and built. It had three blocks, a teacher's staff room and students filled the classrooms.

FIGHTING GENDER BIAS

Creating something new is always a challenge. But to do so as a Ugandan woman made things even harder and Beatrice faced strong gender bias from her community, competitors and even her family.

Her own uncles tried to rally her siblings and father against her arguing that women in Uganda were not supposed to own any property or be independent. Yet, this made her father even more determined to see Beatrice succeed.

When registering the school, local officers did not attend to her request. She asked her husband to intervene. He did and she gave him a 50% shareholding in the school.

Overcoming these challenges was worth it as the number of new applications swelled. But Beatrice needed support. The local bank directed her to attend the Empretec training workshop.

Here she learned human resources management, accounting, diversification, competitiveness, and most importantly, her rights as a businesswoman. Empretec workshop helped her operate her business in a more structured manner, leading to her 2010 Empretec Women in Business award and giving her great international exposure.

She received grants from people who visited the school and got an opportunity to attend a study tour at the University of Texas. Many people were inspired to extend their support to teaching and guiding her teaching staff.

THE DENOUEMENT

Unfortunately, Beatrice fell behind on payments and her competitors used her divorce as the reason to sabotage her school, she says. She decided to sell the school.

Still an evergreen entrepreneur, she wasn't deterred by the failure. She turned her land site into a marketplace, called the Beatrice Hope Foundation, for women to sell vegetables. "Be passionate and face challenges with grace. They help to make you a better person so work on them and improvise. Start small and think big," she advises.

FIND OUT MORE

https://twitter.com/BeatriceAyuru
https://www.linkedin.com/in/beatrice-ayuru-74b21427/

Notes